THE WORLD BANK GROUP, THE IMF AND HUMAN RIGHTS

THE WORLD BANK GROUP, THE IMF AND HUMAN RIGHTS

A Contextualised Way Forward

Willem van Genugten

intersentia
Cambridge – Antwerp – Portland

Intersentia Ltd
Sheraton House | Castle Park
Cambridge | CB3 0AX | United Kingdom
Tel.: +44 1223 370 170 | Email: mail@intersentia.co.uk

Distribution for the UK:
NBN International
Airport Business Centre, 10 Thornbury Road
Plymouth, PL6 7 PP
United Kingdom
Tel.: +44 1752 202 301 | Fax: +44 1752 202 331
Email: orders@nbninternational.com

Distribution for the USA and Canada:
International Specialized Book Services
920 NE 58th Ave. Suite 300
Portland, OR 97213
USA
Tel.: +1 800 944 6190 (toll free)
Email: info@isbs.com

Distribution for Austria:
Neuer Wissenschaftlicher Verlag
Argentinierstraße 42/6
1040 Wien
Austria
Tel.: +43 1 535 61 03 24
Email: office@nwv.at

Distribution for other countries:
Intersentia Publishing nv
Groenstraat 31
2640 Mortsel
Belgium
Tel.: +32 3 680 15 50
Email: mail@intersentia.be

The World Bank Group, the IMF and Human Rights. A Contextualised Way Forward
Willem van Genugten

Artwork on cover: Circle of four colors according to Ostwald (Vierteiliger farbkreis nach Ostwald), anonymous student of the Bauhaus School Dessau/Berlin. Photographic reproduction © Centre Pompidou, MNAM-CCI, Dist. RMN-Grand Palais / Jacques Faujour

ISBN 978-1-78068-296-9
D/2015/7849/35
NUR 828

British Library Cataloguing in Publication Data. A catalogue record for this book is available from the British Library.

PREFACE

In 2009, the Steering Committee for the programme 'Beyond Territoriality: Globalisation and Transnational Human Rights Obligations' (GLOTHRO), funded by the European Science Foundation and led by Belgian Professor Wouter Vandenhole, started a project on the human rights obligations of international financial institutions, most notably the International Monetary Fund (IMF) and the World Bank Group (WBG), which is composed of the International Bank for Reconstruction and Development (IBRD), the International Finance Corporation (IFC), the International Development Association (IDA), the Multilateral Investment Guarantee Agency (MIGA), and the International Centre for Settlement of Investment Disputes (ICSID). The project would build on a previous project, started in 2001 by the present author, which led to the publication of *World Bank, IMF and Human Rights* in 2003, containing the 'Tilburg Guiding Principles on the World Bank Group, the IMF and Human Rights'.[1]

The present publication provides an extensive explanatory text to, and a make-over of, the 2003 Guiding Principles, now called the 'Tilburg-GLOTHRO Guiding Principles on the World Bank Group, the IMF and Human Rights' (see Annex I). These principles are adapted to new insights and developments in the domain of international human rights law over the last decade, with special emphasis on the extraterritoriality of human rights, as well as on developments taking place in the domain of the international legal responsibilities of international organisations and their Member States. The text does *not* discuss the extent to which the WBG and IMF, and other multilateral development banks to which the findings would apply *mutatis mutandis*, actually live up to their international human rights legal obligations in daily practice. The focus is on discussing and clarifying the underlying legal concepts.

The explanatory text is comprised of arguments substantiating the Guiding Principles, taken either from doctrine or legal authorities. The aim of the publication is to clarify by what norms of international human rights law the WBG, IMF, and other IFIs are bound in 2014. Both the Guiding Principles and the text are meant to (re)present the relevant existing international human rights law (*de lege lata*), while adding a number of

1 Willem van Genugten, Paul Hunt and Susan Mathews (eds), *World Bank, IMF and Human Rights*, Nijmegen: Wolf Legal Publishers, 2003.

proposals with a view to the future law (*de lege ferenda*). The text is presented in a way that should be accessible, perhaps sometimes with determination, to non-IFI specialists. For this reason, legal technicalities have occasionally been rephrased in simpler terms, with care to retain their legal accuracy. The number of references is also kept to a minimum. Footnotes are used only in conjunction with direct quotes and in a few other cases, such as when referring to specific legal sources. A short bibliography at the end provides a number of core publications consulted during the project and relevant for further reading.

The format and text of the Principles were discussed at workshops at Tilburg University (20–21 April 2012) and in Geneva (28–29 November 2013), followed by discussions on further integrating the project into the larger aims of the GLOTHRO project at an authors' seminar in Antwerp (3–4 February 2014) and in the final GLOTHRO conference in Turku (27–29 March 2014). These meetings were attended by a range of people; some of them contributed by delivering text blocks or orally, and their contributions were used to revise the successive drafts. This relates most notably to *Wolfgang Benedek, Josh Curtis, Charline Daelman, Asbjørn Eide, Mary Footer, Ann Sofia Freitas de Barros, Tara van Ho, Yannick Radi, Cedric Ryngaert, Sigrun Skogly, Arne Vandenbogaerde*, and *Wouter Vandenhole.*

Over the course of the project a range of other people also participated in one way or another and influenced my thinking on the topic(s) discussed. They include: Daniel Augenstein, Andrew Clapham, Koen de Feyter (during the first project, 2001–2003), Cees Flinterman (first project), Bas de Gaay Fortman (first project), Paul Hunt (first project), Nicola Jägers, Jernej Letnar Černič, Ashfaq Khalfan, Cephas Lumina, Susan Mathews (first project), Ruth Okediji, Camilo Pérez Bustillo (first project), Martin Scheinin, Ian Seiderman and Alfredo Sfeir-Younis (first project). Still others were not available to participate, but contributed strongly to the outcome of the project through their writing. See the bibliography and, more particularly, the authors referred to in the footnotes.

Having said that, it must be made clear that none of the persons mentioned above bear any responsibility for the final text; all shortcuts, unfinished arguments and mistakes are mine. Stating this is not a matter of false modesty: the domain is huge and complex, and the alternative would have been to write a lengthy handbook. *Quod non.*

Willem van Genugten
Tilburg, December 2014

CONTENTS

LIST OF ABBREVIATIONS

CAO	Compliance Advisor/Ombudsman (World Bank Group)
CESCR	Committee on Economic, Social and Cultural Rights
DARIO	Draft Articles on the Responsibility of International Organizations
DARS	Draft Articles on the Responsibility of States for Internationally Wrongful Acts
GLOTHRO	Globalisation and Transnational Human Rights Obligations
HRIA	human rights impact assessments
IEO	Independent Evaluation Office (IMF)
IFC	International Finance Corporation
IFI	international financial institution
IMF	International Monetary Fund
MDB	multilateral development banks
MIGA	Multilateral Investment Guarantee Agency
NGO	non-governmental organisation
OECD	Organisation for Economic Co-operation and Development
PCA	Permanent Court of Arbitration
UN	United Nations
UNGPs	UN Guiding Principles on Business and Human Rights
WBG	World Bank Group

CHAPTER 1
INTRODUCTION

Are the World Bank Group (WBG) and the International Monetary Fund (IMF) bound to abide by international human rights law? For many legal and non-legal specialists it is clear that human rights must not be treated as something separate from activities conducted by the United Nations (UN) and the international organisations attached to, and closely working with, the UN. This is referred to as the 'mainstreaming of human rights'. In this approach, the concept of human rights is used as a bridge in the fight against the (over-)fragmentation of international law and as a (the) guiding principle for the composite and complex organisation called the United Nations. This approach applies international human rights laws to the main organs of the UN and all the international organisations and specialised bodies linked to the UN, such as, in the context of the present publication, the WBG and the IMF. Others, however, argue that the charters and other constitutive documents of these international financial institutions (IFIs) have to be honoured and that one has to respect their specialisations. The consequence of this argument would be that such charters could/should be placed above or, at least, alongside other international obligations that the IFIs have by virtue of their links to the 'UN family'. Both views keep coming up in discussions on the questions why and to what extent the WBG and IMF are legally bound by international human rights standards. The key aim of the present publication is to make it clear by what norms of international human rights law both the WBG and the IMF are bound, and to further identify and specify points for coining their responsibility for violating these norms. As to the latter, the focus is on principles and concepts that can help to attribute and apportion such responsibility to these IFIs, including the responsibility shared with their Member States.

As to the terminology used, the 2001 *Draft Articles on the Responsibility of States for Internationally Wrongful Acts* (DARS) use the term 'attribution of conduct' to a State (Article 2, header of Chapter II and Articles 10 and 11). The 2011 *Draft Articles on the Responsibility of International Organizations* (DARIO) do the same in relation to international organisations (Article 4, header of Chapter II and Article 9). On the other hand, the 2012 *Maastricht Principles on Extraterritorial Obligations of States in the Area of Economic, Social and Cultural Rights* (Maastricht ETO Principles) speak about 'the attribution of State responsibility for the conduct of…' (header, Principle 12) and Principle 11 states that 'State responsibility is engaged as a result of conduct attributable to a state…'. My approach is that the facts have to be established first; the next step is to see whether or not the facts reveal human rights violations, and if so, which one(s) specifically; the third step is to establish who bears the responsibility for these violations and will have to accept the consequences thereof. For these reasons I use wordings such as 'concepts that can help to attribute unlawful conduct and apportion the corresponding responsibility' and 'the attribution of unlawful conduct and the establishment of the corresponding responsibility'.

The first wording addresses the way that both the WBG and the IMF themselves identify the overlap between their respective fields of operation and human rights issues, which is covered in Chapter 2 of this publication. Chapter 3 elaborates on the human rights obligations of both of these IFIs and their Member States. Chapter 4 discusses the responsibility for human rights violations by IFIs and their Member States. Chapter 5 addresses the issues of accountability and redress, followed by some concluding remarks in Chapter 6.

CHAPTER 2

IFIs POSITIONING THEMSELVES IN THE HUMAN RIGHTS FIELD

Before addressing the obligations following from existing international human rights law as it relates to the WBG and the IMF, this chapter illustrates how both of these IFIs present themselves today in relation to the links between their respective mandates and international human rights. This is undertaken to make it clear that discussing the obligations following from existing human rights law and the attribution of conduct that violates these norms in Chapters 3 and 4 is not a matter of imposing something externally upon IFIs, but links to discussions underway in both IFIs.

2.1. OFFICIAL WBG POSITION

The WBG underlines in its own recent policy statements that internal developments have shown 'growing recognition of the need for the Bank to address human rights in a more explicit fashion' and that there 'have been significant advances in the Bank's thinking on this issue'.[2] The evidence provided relates to the Bank's pronouncements from as early as 1998 on human rights, which contained statements about how the Bank supports the realisation of human rights and how it believes that 'creating the conditions for the attainment of human rights is a central and irreducible goal of development'.[3] The Bank's official statements refer to several developments outside the Bank, such as the 2003 *UN Common Understanding on a Human Rights Based Approach to Development*; the Secretary General's 2005 report *In Larger Freedom*; and the findings of the 2006 World Development Report *Equity and Development*. In the words of the Bank, '[t]he World Development Report 2006 explores the ways in which structural and distributional inequalities can hinder development, and grounds equity in

---

2 See: http://web.worldbank.org/WBSITE/EXTERNAL/EXTSITETOOLS/0,,contentMDK:20749693~pagePK:98400~piPK:98424~theSitePK:95474,00.html#1. This website refers to underlying publications of the WBG, some of which will be referred to again in the remainder of this article.

3 *Ibidem*; no page number available.

two basic principles: Equality of opportunity and the avoidance of absolute deprivation, both of which have human rights dimensions'.[4] Further to this, the Bank refers to, *inter alia*, its cooperation with the Office of the High Commissioner of Human Rights on several initiatives including, for example, supporting countries to take human rights considerations into account in the preparation of their poverty reduction strategies, as well as with the Organisation for Economic Co-operation and Development (OECD) Development Assistance Committee (DAC). On a practical note, the Bank adds that:

> although its policies, programs and projects have never been explicitly or deliberately aimed towards the realization of human rights, the Bank contributes to the promotion of human rights in different areas, e.g., improving poor people's access to health, education, food and water; promoting the participation of indigenous peoples in decision-making and the accountability of governments to their citizens; supporting justice reforms; fighting corruption; and increasing transparency of governments.[5]

In addition, the Bank explicitly states that 'there are wide areas of overlap between substantive areas covered by core human rights treaties and those areas in which the Bank operates'.[6] Further to that, while reflecting on 'the way forward', the Bank speaks of 'recognizing the role of human rights as legal principles, which may inform a broad range of policies and activities'. Even more directly, the Bank speaks of:

> understanding human rights as actionable legal obligations, in certain circumstances and under certain conditions, such as those arising from international treaties, or as they are enshrined in national laws, where the Bank's role is to support its members to fulfill those obligations where they relate to World Bank projects and policies.[7]

This terminology approaches the legal terminology used in Chapters 3 and 4 of the present publication and overlaps with the beginning of the legal reasoning developed in these chapters. Despite the restriction 'in certain circumstances and under certain conditions', the progressive message the Bank sends to the outside world is clear. The Bank goes even further

4 *Ibidem.*
5 *Ibidem.*
6 *Ibidem.*
7 *Ibidem.*

by stating that 'our partners in the broader UN family have *a comparative advantage* in this area. Unlike the WBG, many of them [UN agencies] have mandates that contain an explicit commitment to human rights, including, in some cases, monitoring and enforcement capabilities' (emphasis added).[8] In other words, the WBG seems, in some way, to regret that in the past its mandate has not been explicitly linked to human rights, a fact that would have made its current work easier or given it a 'comparative advantage' in a sense.

Formulating its position this way, the Bank shows a clear openness to the human rights domain and even acknowledges the practical utility of being linked to human rights norms and even human rights enforcement mechanisms. It should be added, however, that the quotes presented here are still rather empty from a legal point of view, despite the strong terminology chosen. The same goes for the link between the words chosen and the outside world. The latter, however, is not the focus of the present publication. The way the WBG *presents itself* to the outside world, however, will be used to further confront the WBG with its human rights obligations and the consequences thereof.

2.2. OFFICIAL IMF POSITION

Many issues the IMF is dealing with are directly related to human rights. However, it is well known that, compared to the WBG, the IMF is even less pronounced on linking such activities to obligations stemming from international human rights law. Whether that position is tenable will be discussed in the later chapters. For now, the focus is on the wording chosen by the IMF to illustrate the overlap in substance between the two domains.

In a number of IMF publications over the last decade, one can find numerous references to human rights. A good example is a 2010 IMF Staff Position Note on *The Human Cost of Recessions: Assessing it, Reducing it*, prepared by the Research Department of the IMF.[9] To take but one quote from this Note on the impact of economic recessions on children:

> The short and long-run costs of unemployment do not appear to be limited to the individual or generation directly affected. Several studies have found that

8 *Ibidem.*

9 Mai Dao and Prakash Loungani, *The Human Cost of Recessions: Assessing it, Reducing it*, Washington: The International Monetary Fund, 2010.

> children of laid-off parents also suffer: in the short-run, parental job loss tends to reduce the schooling achievement of their children.[10]

Although the usual disclaimer is added that 'the views expressed [...] should not be attributed to the IMF, its Executive Board, or its management',[11] the paper is officially authorised for distribution within the IMF and is thus meant, one may assume, to inform IMF policies, programmes and projects, and their drafters. While the words '(human) rights' are not used in the extensive Note, the overlap with the human rights domain is clear, in this particular example, the right of a child to education.

Related statements were made in, for instance, a speech delivered by IMF Managing Director Christine Lagarde during a visit to Malawi in early 2013. While discussing the global and regional economic context, she observes, *inter alia*, that one should:

> not forget the threat from food prices and food scarcity. So far, rising global food price pressures are concentrated in a few crops like maize, soybeans, and wheat. But drought and crop failure are becoming ever-present dangers in some areas, with grave consequences for livelihoods and even lives.[12]

Other remarks made by Lagarde in this particular speech relate to looking at 'improving human development' by seeing economic growth as 'a means to a higher end: Creating the conditions for the flourishing of human potential'. In that context, she quotes Malawi President Banda:

> Growth is not merely GDP growth. Growth is about wealth and prosperity for all, opportunity for all, happiness for all, political and economic freedom for all. Growth is also about growing the number of children in school, and young people in jobs. Growth is about increasing the number of mothers who give safe birth in a hospital, and growing the number of families who have plenty of food.[13]

The links to human rights are extremely clear, from political freedom to the right to education, from the right to adequate healthcare to the right to food.

---

10 *Ibidem*, p. 7.

11 *Ibidem*, front page.

12 Christine Lagarde, 'Malawi – Economic Rebirth, Renewed Partnerships', speech delivered on 5 January 2013 in Lilongwe, Malawi, available at: https://www.imf.org/external/np/speeches/2013/010513.htm.

13 *Ibidem*.

The quotes taken from this speech would not be misplaced in a document devoted to the key social goal behind human rights law: the realisation of a life of human dignity for all human beings worldwide, more particularly in the context of the present publication, for those human beings living in the countries with which the IMF has a working relationship.

As a follow-up to the latter quote, Lagarde touches upon the progress Malawi has made in areas such as reducing child mortality, combating deadly diseases like HIV/AIDS and malaria, ensuring environmental sustainability, and strengthening global partnerships for development, while, according to her, progress is lagging in other vital areas, such as the eradication of extreme poverty, attaining universal primary education, promoting gender equality and empowering women, and improving maternal health. All these are human rights (related) issues, which are mainly in the domain of economic and social rights, but also extend beyond these rights, such as the issue of gender equality. Lagarde's approach illustrates her awareness of the key links between an economic and financial focus and the long-term goals of the IMF's programmes, *i.e.* creating – or helping States and their inhabitants to create (*i.e.* empowering) – economic and social environments within which human rights can flourish.

In another speech, also delivered in 2013, Lagarde describes the future direction of the organisation.[14] Doing so, she touches upon a number of 'new frontiers of risk' for the IMF, such as the fact that by 2030 there will be 1.1 billion more people in the world than today, that 97 per cent of them will be living in emerging and developing countries, and that one billion people will be 65 years or older: 'These demographics and their inter-generational costs will dramatically affect education, healthcare, savings, pensions, public spending.'[15] Further to that, Lagarde says that:

> Average temperatures are rising, and with it the risk of more frequent natural disasters, more volatile agricultural output, and more food and water insecurity. In many countries, particularly the poorest, it will exacerbate their already fragile state.[16]

---

14 Christine Lagarde, 'The Future Global Economy and the Future Fund', speech delivered on 11 October 2013 in Washington DC, available at: https://www.imf.org/external/np/speeches/2013/101113.htm.

15 *Ibidem.*

16 *Ibidem.*

Lagarde observes, however, that the IMF should 'not stray into the mandates of other organizations'.[17] This comment links to the argument presented above concerning the honouring of charters and other constitutive documents of international organisations and respecting their specialisations (and one might assume that Lagarde had 'vice versa' in mind when stating this), but that this should not bar effective cooperation 'with the Bank and others, drawing on their expertise as needed, and offering ours'.[18]

As to all these areas, Lagarde states in her speech that the IMF's comparative advantage is its macro-economic perspective and that '[m]aintaining that focus and adapting our approach is what has made the IMF an effective institution in the past'.[19] Taking all the foregoing together one can conclude that the IMF is slightly re-positioning itself in the midst of major global problems. This is of course what international organisations do regularly and, as 'living' organisations, should do continuously – in other words, such organisations should keep looking for options to make their mandates and actual activities optimally relevant, given the changes in the realities they have to face and in the ways these realities are seen and conceptualised. The above quoted IMF Staff Note and the speeches by IMF Managing Director Lagarde fit in this perspective and further clarify the links between the IMF's key domain (to which it rightly wants to stick) and the human rights field. It should be emphasised, however, that the IMF does not yet attract the legal consequences of international human rights law. In addition, it must be observed that neither internal staff notes nor speeches given by the IMF Managing Director necessarily reflect the mainstream view of the organisation. Nevertheless, it is reasonable to assume that the quotes taken from these recent IMF documents at least reflect aspects of an ongoing debate of direct relevance to the place of human rights within the work of the IMF. And, as observed in relation to the WBG, the IMF cannot afford to use such words for free.

---

17 *Ibidem.*

18 *Ibidem.*

19 *Ibidem.*

CHAPTER 3
APPLICABLE HUMAN RIGHTS OBLIGATIONS

3.1. INTRODUCTION

As subjects of international law and as international legal personalities, the WBG and the IMF are capable of possessing rights and duties under their constituent instruments, general rules of international law, and the treaties to which they have acceded. This includes obligations in the domain of human rights, to be exercised separately from, or jointly with, their Member States. This statement will be further substantiated in this chapter by scrutinising the links between the mandates of IFIs and international human rights law (subsection 3.2); the incorporation of IFIs in the domain of international human rights law (subsection 3.3); the 'political prohibition', which prevents the WBG from interfering in political affairs (subsection 3.4); the human rights obligations of States acting in the context of IFIs (subsection 3.5); and the obligations following from the (legal) relationships between IFIs and private subcontractors (subsection 3.6).

3.2. THE LINKS BETWEEN IFI MANDATES AND INTERNATIONAL HUMAN RIGHTS LAW

As explained in Chapter 2, the WBG has chosen not to interpret its mandate in isolation from developments taking place in the human rights domain, while sometimes touching upon legal terminology. The IMF also 'plays' with human rights terminology, albeit in a different way. The question is which more specific human rights obligations can be linked to the mandates of these organisations and on what grounds. Let me first borrow the enlightening words of Mac Darrow – the author of a seminal book on the issue in 2003[20] – used by him in a piece written in 2009 for the renowned *Encyclopedia of Human Rights*:[21]

> The UN Charter is perhaps the most important source of human rights duties for members of the extended UN family; the UN Charter binds the bank and the IMF equally. The IBRD [International Bank for Reconstruction and Development], IDA [International Development Association], and IMF have all entered into formal relationship agreements with the UN. The promotion of human rights is at the heart of the UN system's purposes, as provided in articles 1(3) and 55 of the UN Charter, although specific obligations are not well-defined. However, the Universal Declaration of Human Rights (1948), and to some extent subsequent international human rights treaties enjoying broad acceptance and are viewed by many as an elaboration or authoritative interpretation of the brief human rights references in the UN Charter. Taking the relevant provisions of the UN Charter as a whole, it is strongly arguable that cooperation between the BWIs [Bretton Woods Institutions] and the UN in the economic and social fields should be based, at least in part, on the UN Charter's human rights principles.[22]

This links to, and further specifies, what has been stated above on human rights in general. Darrow adds in the same piece, correct to my mind, that:

> [m]ainstream international legal opinion would say that this translates into a minimum obligation that the Bank and the IMF respect (or at least not violate) human rights commitments in force in member countries and arguably also protect human rights within the scope of their influence and activities at the country level.[23]

In addition, according to him, '[m]any commentators go further still to argue that these institutions should promote or perhaps even fulfill human rights'.[24] Having said that, Darrow also refers to the often cited 2006 *Legal Opinion on Human Rights and the Work of the World Bank*, by the Bank's

---

20 Mac Darrow, *Between Light and Shadow; The World Bank, The International Monetary Fund and International Human Rights Law*, Oxford: Hart Publishing, 2003.

21 Mac Darrow, 'World and International Monetary Fund', in: David Forsythe (Editor in Chief), *Encyclopedia of Human Rights*, Vol. 5, Oxford: Oxford University Press, 2009 ff, pp. 373–381.

22 *Ibidem*, p. 378.

23 *Ibidem.*

24 *Ibidem.*

General Counsel at the time, Roberto Dañino.[25] This Legal Opinion, written at the request of the Bank's senior management,[26] is labelled by Darrow and others as a 'watershed' and was a:

> marked departure from the conservative doctrine of the 1980s and 1990s, this legal opinion posited a purposive and contextual interpretation of the Articles of Agreement, setting out an enabling framework for the Bank to grapple explicitly with human rights issues arising within the increasingly broad and complex sphere of its operations and support its members in realizing their human rights obligations. Strikingly the opinion concluded that the Articles of Agreement permit, and in some cases require, the Bank to recognize the human rights dimension of its development policies and activities, since it is now evident that human rights are an intrinsic part of the Bank's mission.[27]

The legal opinion has not been brought before the Bank's Executive Board, but, according to Darrow, the 'persuasive effect of the opinion does not depend on the board's endorsement, although to formally bind the bank's operations the key provisions of the opinion would need to be reflected in the bank's operational policies, which do require such approval', and that is 'not a likely prospect'.[28] One can agree with the latter comment, although this also depends on the timeframe one has in mind. I would agree with Darrow's remark as far as it relates to the present and maybe the immediately foreseeable future, but things can and will change. In any case, it can be observed that whether or not the 2006 Legal Opinion was a real watershed, things are gradually changing within the World Bank and are not carved in stone.

The Bank's next General Counsel, Ana Palacio, stated that the 2006 Legal Opinion 'marks a clear evolution from the pre-existing restrictive legal interpretation of the Bank's explicit consideration of human rights', but she reads it as 'permissive: allowing, but not mandating, action on the part of the Bank in relation to human rights'.[29] The word 'permissive'

---

25 Also see Roberto Daniño, 'The Legal Aspects of the World Bank's Work on Human Rights: Some Preliminary Thoughts', in: Philip Alston and Mary Robinson (eds), *Human Rights and Development: Towards Mutual Reinforcement*, Oxford: Oxford University Press, 2005, *passim*.

26 See Ana Palacio, *The Way Forward; Human Rights and the World Bank*, World Bank Institute, Special Report Development Outreach, Washington, 2006, p. 36.

27 Mac Darrow, *supra* n. 21, p. 378.

28 *Ibidem*, p. 379.

29 Ana Palacio, *supra* n. 26, p. 36.

creates space for the Bank to act according to its own views on human rights issues and/or legal obligations. Later on, this space will be further tested. Palacio herself adds that the 2006 Legal Opinion clarifies 'the state of the law' and that it 'gives the Bank the necessary leeway to explore its proper role in relation to human rights, updating the legal stance adopted internally to accord with the Bank's practice and the current international legal context'.[30] She also notes that it is clear that human rights 'can and sometimes should' be taken into consideration by the Bank as part of its decision-making process, amongst other things through the 'recognition of the role of human rights as *legal principles* [italics in the original text] which may inform a broad range of activities, and which may enrich the quality and rationale of development interventions'.[31] A few years later, Siobhán McInerney-Lankford and Hans-Otto Sano observed, in a study done for the World Bank and the Nordic Trust Fund, that despite such developments the official approach of the World Bank with regard to human rights 'remains non-explicit in terms of the direct or formal relevance of specific duties or international treaty obligations'.[32] This still reflects the situation in 2014 and shows how the WBG 'plays' around the legal obligations part of the human rights field.

As for the IMF, one can refer to a range of publications by, amongst others, the former General Counsel, François Gianviti. He has explicitly reflected on the 'non-links' between the IMF and human rights law, more particularly the International Covenant on Economic, Social and Cultural Rights. Gianviti points out:

> There are three reasons for concluding that the Covenant does not apply to the Fund: the Fund is not a party to the Covenant; the obligations imposed by the Covenant apply only to States, not to international organizations; and the Covenant, in its Article 24, explicitly recognizes that '[n]othing in the present Covenant shall be interpreted as impairing the provisions [...] of the constitutions of the specialized agencies which define the respective responsibilities [...] of the specialized agencies in regard to the matters dealt with in the present Covenant'.[33]

---

30 *Ibidem.*

31 *Ibidem.*

32 Siobhán McInerney-Lankford and Hans-Otto Sano, *Human Rights Indicators in Development*, Washington: World Bank & the Nordic Trust Fund, 2010, p. 6.

33 François Gianviti, General Council IMF (1987–2004), 'Economic, Social and Cultural Rights and the International Monetary Fund', 2002, available

In addition, Gianviti discusses the often heard argument that 'the obligations set forth in the Covenant are mandatory provisions of general public international law and, thus, binding on all subjects of international law, including international organizations' and that this must lead to the conclusion 'that the Fund's Articles of Agreement should be interpreted in a manner consistent with the objective of promoting the rights contained in the Covenant, or deemed to be amended if this was necessary to achieve these objectives'.[34] Gianviti concludes that if the principle is admitted, 'the Covenant takes precedence over the Articles [of Agreement], the whole institutional and legal structure within which the Fund operates can be questioned'.[35] With this statement he clearly tries to escape the binding force of international human rights obligations.

Even a more moderate view of the links between the IMF and human rights, one in which the IMF has to take human rights, more specifically the International Covenant on Economic, Social and Cultural Rights, into consideration is not embraced by him. One of his key arguments is that the IMF is not a UN body and is not bound by general UN/international law: the IMF is 'an intergovernmental agency, not an agency of the United Nations'.[36] He observes that in accordance with Article 57 of the UN Charter, the IMF was brought into relationship with the United Nations by an agreement in which the United Nations recognises that, 'by reason of the nature of its international responsibilities and the terms of its Articles of Agreement, the Fund is, and is required to function as, an independent organization'.[37] And most importantly:

> Article X of the Fund's Articles of Agreement, while requiring the Fund to cooperate with 'any general international organization' [i.e. the United Nations], specifies that 'Any arrangements for such cooperation which would involve a modification of any provision of [the Articles of Agreement] may be effected only after amendment to [the Articles]'.[38]

at: www.imf.org/external/np/leg/sem/2002/cdmfl/eng/gianv3.pdf, *passim*, esp. paras. 6, 16 and 60.

34 *Ibidem*, para. 14.

35 *Ibidem*.

36 *Ibidem*, para. 16.

37 *Ibidem*.

38 *Ibidem*.

This led Gianviti to the conclusion that the relationship between the IMF and the UN is not one of 'agency', but one of 'sovereign equals'.[39] This sovereignty issue will be discussed in subsection 3.4.

Darrow observes in relation to the IMF's Articles of Agreement that '[t]he ability, or obligation, of the IMF to consider human rights issues in connection with its work depends to a lesser degree than that of the bank upon the question of how its Articles of Agreement should be interpreted' and how its wishes to use and actually uses its 'implied powers'.[40] And, thus, Darrow points out that, 'perhaps surprisingly, the IMF's Articles [of Agreement] are relatively permissive in scope compared with those of the bank, and they contain no equivalent of the political prohibition [...] that for so long dogged efforts to breathe life into the bank's constitution'.[41] For now, the key question is to what extent the WBG and the IMF can be 'ordered', based on developments in the human rights field and in general international law, to accept direct human obligations and use their positions to address human rights issues as part of their mandates.

3.3. INCORPORATING IFIs IN THE DOMAIN OF INTERNATIONAL HUMAN RIGHTS LAW

Is the space that the WBG and the IMF are creating for themselves still justifiable? One can discern several aspects of international human rights law and general international law that are directly applicable to both of these IFIs. They are mentioned here in a schematic and non-exhaustive way, with limited references.

Firstly, both IFIs are necessarily bound by those human rights standards that qualify as peremptory standards of international law (*ius cogens*), such as the obligation to refrain from (aiding and abetting) genocide, torture, and racial discrimination and the obligation to respect and actively protect the right to self-determination of peoples. Secondly, IFIs are bound by general principles of international (human rights) law, such as the obligation to make reparation in the case of an internationally wrongful act and the principle of due diligence as coined amongst other things in

39 *Ibidem.*
40 Darrow, *supra* n. 21, p. 379.
41 *Ibidem.*

the context of human rights,[42] and by customary international law rules in the domain of human rights, such as the obligations following from certain human rights conventions of the International Labour Organization (ILO), representing norms of an international customary law character: C29, on Forced Labour (1930); C87, on Freedom of Association and Protection of the Right to Organise (1948); C98, on the Right to Organise and Collective Bargaining (1949); C100, on Equal Remuneration (1951); C105, on Abolition of Forced Labour (1957); C111, on Discrimination ([in the context of] Employment and Occupation) (1958); C138, on Minimum Age (1973); and C182, on Worst Forms of Child Labour (1999).

Thirdly, as Specialized Agencies of the UN, which have entered into relationship agreements with the UN Economic and Social Council in accordance with Articles 57 and 63 of the UN Charter, the IMF and WBG are bound to respect the principles and objectives of the UN, even though especially the IMF has occasionally retained the right to be seen independently from the UN as well.[43] One can agree with the observation by the International Law Commission, made in the context of its extensive studies on the fragmentation of international law, that the term 'self-contained regime', often also used by and for the IFIs to justify their special position, is 'a misnomer' and that '[n]o legal regime is isolated from general international law'.[44]

---

42 See for instance the wording by Human Rights Watch, used in *Abuse-Free Development: How the World Bank Should Safeguard Against Human Rights Violations*, New York, July 2013: 'Ongoing due diligence should include continually identifying and analysing human rights risks throughout the course of a project and require the Bank to publicly acknowledge the human rights risks.' Also see the wording chosen in the Dutch Action Plan on Business and Human Rights, summarising UN Guiding Principle on Business and Human Rights no. 17: 'Due diligence may be defined as follows: Identifying and assessing human rights impacts: taking proactive, ongoing steps to understand how existing and proposed activities may cause or contribute to human rights impacts. Taking action and tracking effectiveness of response. Externally communicating how the business has addressed adverse impacts: it is possible that these impacts are not the direct result of a business's own operations, but are caused elsewhere within the supply chain. Due diligence is not a one-off activity but an ongoing process.' The Hague, April 2014, p. 21.

43 See, most clearly and explicitly: François Gianviti, *supra* n. 33, esp. paras. 6, p. 16 and p. 60.

44 Report of the Study Group of the International Law Commission, finalised by Martti Koskenniemi, 'Fragmentation of International Law: Difficulties Arising

Fourthly, there are many relevant pronouncements, both within certain treaties and emanating from particular supervisory bodies in the domain of human rights, that include the IFIs within the juridical domain of international human rights law. Especially certain General Comments by the Committee on Economic, Social and Cultural Rights (CESCR) provide specific examples. In its 2002 General Comment on the right to water, for instance, the CESCR notes that:

> [t]he international financial institutions, notably the International Monetary Fund (IMF) and the World Bank, should take into account the right to water in their lending policies, credit agreements, structural adjustment programmes and other development projects […], so that the enjoyment of the right to water is promoted.[45]

Stating so, the CESCR addresses the IFIs themselves. In other General Comments, it addresses the Member States of both IFIs. In its 2008 General Comment on social security, for instance, the CESCR observes that 'States parties should ensure that their actions as members of international organizations take due account of the right to social security' and that:

> [a]ccordingly, States parties that are members of international financial institutions, notably the International Monetary Fund, the World Bank, and regional development banks, should take steps to ensure that the right to social security is taken into account in their lending policies, credit agreements and other international measures.[46]

Such General Comments are not binding upon States, but, summarising a long debate, one can agree with Conway Blake that General Comments are 'a testament to the dynamic nature of international law and its institutions' and that, while their authority 'cannot be viewed in traditional legal terms', they 'emerge as an authoritative interpretation, which gives rise to normative consensus on the meaning and scope of particular human rights'.[47]

---

from the Diversification and Expansion of International Law', UN Doc. A/CN.4/L.682, 13 April 2006, para. 193.

45 UN Doc. E/C.12/GC/15, 20 January 2003, para. 60.

46 UN Doc E/C.12/GC/19, 4 February 2008, para. 58.

47 Conway Blake, 'Normative Instruments in International Human Rights Law: Locating the General Comment', Center for Human Rights and Global Justice Working Paper Number 17, New York, 2008, p. 38.

A fifth aspect relates to the concept of 'the right to development', as laid down, *inter alia*, in the 1986 Declaration on the Right to Development.[48] Despite its perhaps limited legal value,[49] the Declaration, as well as the concept of development as such, still serves as a semi-legal (soft law) and practical tool for especially human rights advocacy.[50] In addition, there is no misunderstanding of the relevance of the concept of 'development' to the mandates of both the WBG and the IMF. Illustrating this point, one can refer to, for instance, the view of both of these IFIs themselves on the need to help realise the 2000 Millennium Declaration, including the eight Millennium Development Goals, many of which directly relate to human rights.[51]

3.4. THE 'POLITICAL PROHIBITION' ON THE WORLD BANK

Discussing the manifold relations between the mandates of the IFIs and human rights, one also enters the domain of the so-called 'political prohibition', used by the WBG. Article IV, Section 10, of the World Bank's Articles of Agreement provide that '[t]he Bank and its officers shall not interfere in the political affairs of any member; nor shall they be influenced in their decisions by the political character of the member or members concerned', and that '[o]nly economic considerations shall be relevant to their decisions'.[52] The inclusion of this 'political prohibition' relates to the

48 UN Doc. A/RES/31/128, 4 December 1986.

49 See: Arne Vandenbogaerde, 'The Right to Development in International Human Rights Law: a Call for its Dissolution', *Netherlands Quarterly of Human Rights*, Vol. 31/2, 2013, pp. 187–209.

50 In the same vain: Olajumoke O. Oduwole, 'International Law and the Right to Development: A Pragmatic Approach For Africa', Inaugural Lecture as Professor to the Prince Claus Chair in Development and Equity 2013/2015 delivered on 20 May 2014 at the International Institute of Social Studies, The Hague, the Netherlands, p. 3.

51 See recently, 'The IMF and the Millennium Development Goals', IMF Factsheet (2014), available at: https://www.imf.org/external/np/exr/facts/pdf/mdg.pdf. Also see the successive annual World Bank and IMF Global Monitoring Reports (so far: 2004–2013), Washington, DC: World Bank, and World Bank & OECD; and: OECD and World Bank, *Integrating Human Rights into Development: Donor Approaches, Experiences, and Challenges* (2013, 2nd ed.), Washington, DC.

52 Articles of Agreement, International Bank for Reconstruction and Development, drawn up at the United Nations Monetary and Financial Conference, Bretton Woods, New Hampshire, 1944.

vision of the founders of the Bank for an impartial and neutral institution. The original Articles of Agreement literally forbade the Bank to deal with any issues of a political character, and the Bank considered human rights to be part of that.

The original 'political prohibition' reflected the mainstream thinking on sovereignty and human rights after the end of WWII. As time progressed, in the 1960s 'the Bank understood human rights issues in the context of whether or not it should deal with regimes which had a bad human rights record or were known to commit human rights, usually civil and political rights, violations'.[53] At that time, the Bank also used its Articles 'to fend off criticisms of involvement with such regimes by classifying human rights concerns as "political"'.[54]

However, as discussed above, things are gradually changing; both the IMF and the WBG are now less reluctant or are becoming more willing, be it in different ways and to different degrees, to discuss 'non-economic concerns'. As to the latter wording, one can agree with Adam McBeth that 'the distinction between economic and non-economic matters is artificial and often unsustainable, particularly in placing human rights in the latter, prohibited category'.[55] 'Prohibited' is linked to the domestic affairs of sovereign States. It is well known, however, that large parts of the human rights domain no longer belong to the domestic affairs of States. To mention just a few early markers of that development, one can refer to the 1970 judgement of the International Court of Justice in the Barcelona Traction case, with its famous dictum on *erga omnes* obligations (obligations that are the concern of all States),[56] and to the 1993 Vienna Declaration and Program of Action (that the promotion and protection of all human rights is a legitimate concern of the international community).[57] Other outcomes of lengthy debates – such as the one on Article 48 of DARS,[58] the

---

53 Sanae Fujita, 'The challenges of mainstreaming human rights in the World Bank', *The International Journal of Human Rights*, Vol. 15, No. 3, March 2011, p. 376.

54 *Ibidem*.

55 Adam McBeth, 'A Right by an Other Name: The Evasive Engagement of International Financial Institutions with Human Rights', *The George Washington International Law Review*, Vol. 40, 2009, p. 1110.

56 See: www.icj-cij.org/docket/index.php?p1=3&p2=3&k=1a&case=50&code=bt2&p3=4, paras. 33 and 34.

57 Adopted by the World Conference on Human Rights, Vienna, 1993, available at: www.ohchr.org/EN/ProfessionalInterest/Pages/Vienna.aspx, para. I, 4.

58 An excerpt of the Draft Articles on the Responsibility of States for Internationally Wrongful Acts can be found in Annex II.

Article that relates to the breach of obligations 'owed to the international community as a whole' (Article 48(1)(b), and the one on the Responsibility to Protect, a concept inspired by and based on the move from 'sovereignty as control' to 'sovereignty as responsibility'[59] – build on such notions as well.

In line with, and reflected within, such judgements and documents, a global trend is developing that is asking for another view of sovereignty, being the basic concept behind the 'political prohibition'. This trend is clearly moving away from a rather exclusive focus on State sovereignty ('mind your own business') to a focus on elevating substantive human dignity over certain previously conceived sovereign rights and forms. One does not have to be one of those authors who state that human rights terminology and human rights goals should, and actually already do, permeate (nearly) *all* other domains of international law and policy to see the relevance and actual existence of human rights terminology in other domains of the international law. In a recent article, overall extremely critical of the presumed actual dimensions of the humanisation of the international legal order, Vassilis Tzevelekos comes to the conclusion – after having stripped away all the inflated *de lege ferenda* ('future law') aspects of the humanisation trend – that the obligations *erga omnes (partes)* ('obligations on all States and other actors') and the principle of due diligence are two 'systemic' tools, central to the humanisation of international law. He goes on to say that:

> both these tools form part of modern positive law, but may also make a positive contribution towards the direction of deeper humanisation in international law, having the potential, inter alia, to limit state will, establish occasional material normative hierarchy consisting in conditional priority in the fulfillment of human rights, give a communitarian tone to international law and invite states to be pro-active in the collective protection of their common interests and values.[60]

59 International Commission on Intervention and State Sovereignty, *The Responsibility to Protect, Report of the International Commission*, Ottawa: IDRC, 2001, para. 2.14.

60 Vassilis Tzevelekos, 'Revisiting the Humanisation of International Law: Limits and Potential – Obligations Erga Omnes, Hierarchy of Rules and the Principle of Due Diligence as the Basis for Further Humanisation', *Erasmus Law Review*, Vol. 6, No. 1, 2013, *passim*. The quote is taken from the abstract of the article.

This is a telling way of describing the current state of the humanisation trend. Further to that, Tzevelekos comes to the conclusion that the process of humanisation of the international legal arena needs to be balanced with the decentralised and sovereignist origins of the pluralistic international legal system. I agree with this idea as well as, with the reference to sovereignty and the limits thereto being the key words to my mind.

Applying this to IFIs, and, once again, reacting to Gianviti's interpretation of the IMF Articles of Agreement ending with his remark on 'sovereign equals', one can argue on very solid ground that the respective constitutive Articles of Agreement of both the IMF and the WBG should be seen as dynamic and living instruments, to be interpreted in light of legal developments so far (*de lege lata*) and trends underway (a mix of *de lege lata* and *de lege ferenda*). The latter include the paradigm shift from sovereignty as an inward-looking way of protecting national interests towards sovereignty as co-responsibility for what's going on in the outside world, where problems are no longer 'intra-territorial'.

In light of the foregoing and of current views on human rights extraterritorially, it is clear that the original conceptualisation of the political prohibition is no longer tenable. In addition to the International Law Commission's statement, quoted above, that '[n]o legal regime is isolated from general international law', one can also refer to the Commission's observation that it:

> is hard to see how regime-builders might have agreed not to incorporate (that is, opt out from) such general principles [of international law]. The debate about new states' competence to pick and choose the customary law they wish to apply ended after decolonization without there having been much 'rejection' of old custom. Few actors would care to establish relations with a special regime that claimed a blanket rejection of all general international law. Why, in such case, would anyone (including the regime's establishing members) take the regime's engagements seriously?[61]

The International Law Commission thus calls upon States and, literally as well by implication, their international organisations, to step away from minimalistic approaches to international legal developments. Although this is a *de lege ferenda* call, the substantive arguments in the domain of

61 Report of the Study Group of the International Law Commission, finalised by Martti Koskenniemi, *supra* n. 44, para. 185.

existing international human rights law backing this call cannot be seen as negligible.

3.5. HUMAN RIGHTS OBLIGATIONS OF STATES ACTING IN THE CONTEXT OF IFIs

The IFIs, by their very nature, act transnationally and their Member States, while acting within the framework of the IFIs, do affect the enjoyment of human rights in borrowing States, positively and negatively, and thus act extraterritorially. In addition to what has been said above about the (General Comments of the) CESCR and the obligations of the International Covenant on Economic, Social and Cultural Rights States parties when acting within the WBG and the IMF, the extraterritorial human rights obligations of Member States of international organisations have been given ample attention in, for instance, the 2011 *Maastricht Principles on Extraterritorial Obligations of States in the Area of Economic, Social and Cultural Rights* (Maastricht ETO Principles).[62] According to the Maastricht ETO Principles, these obligations entail a prohibition on direct as well as indirect interference, *i.e.* conduct that 'impairs the ability of another State or international organization to comply with that State's or that international organization's obligations as regards economic, social and cultural rights' (Principle 21) or which 'aids, assists, directs, controls or coerces another State or international organization to breach that State's or that international organization's obligations as regards economic, social and cultural rights, where the former States do so with knowledge of the circumstances of the act' (*ibidem*). In light of general international law, it can be added to the words 'with knowledge...' that ignorance is not always a legitimate defence (more on this aspect and related aspects in subsection 4.2).

In addition, the Maastricht ETO Principles affirm in a number of ways a State's obligation to fulfil human rights. Principle 29, for instance, requires States to take steps 'to create an international enabling environment conducive to the universal fulfilment of economic, social and cultural rights, including in matters relating to bilateral and multilateral trade, investment, taxation, finance, environmental protection, and development cooperation'.

---

62 An excerpt from the Maastricht ETO Principles can be found in Annex II.

Also relevant are the UN Guiding Principles on Business and Human Rights (UNGPs), in particular Principle 10:

> States, when acting as members of multilateral institutions that deal with business related issues, should:
>
> (a) Seek to ensure that those institutions neither restrain the ability of their member States to meet their duty to protect nor hinder business enterprises from respecting human rights;
> (b) Encourage those institutions, within their respective mandates and capacities, to promote business respect for human rights and, where requested, to help States meet their duty to protect against human rights abuse by business enterprises, including through technical assistance, capacity-building and awareness-raising;
> (c) Draw on these Guiding Principles to promote shared understanding and advance international cooperation in the management of business and human rights challenges.[63]

Although one can argue that the UNGPs may not apply equally to all IFI activities and entities, they would in any event cover the International Finance Corporation (IFC), which operates (and finances) together with the private sector. Similarly, there are also issues arising out of the IMF's mandate in terms of its standby arrangements, conditionality policy and aid programmes that call for interaction with corporations and other business enterprises in the borrowing Member States (more on the relationship between both IFIs and the private sector in subsection 3.6).

In addition, it has to be observed that, when considering State participation within IFIs, the executive directors of the IFIs act as representatives of the IFI concerned, but also of the Member State or States that appointed them. It would go beyond the scope of this publication to determine in the present context all possible consequences of these dual capacity acts.[64] However, some IFI Member States have already adopted national human rights legislation imposing certain duties on the executive directors representing them. In the US, a

---

63 An excerpt from the UN Guiding Principles on Business and Human Rights can be found in Annex II.

64 See in much detail: Ana Sofia Barros and Cedric Ryngaert, 'The Position of Member States in (Autonomous) Institutional Decision-Making: Implications for the Establishment of Responsibility', *International Organizations Law Review*, Vol. 11, 2014.

Chapter of the US Code entitled 'Human Rights and United States Assistance policies with international financial institutions' states that 'the United States' government, in connection with its voice and vote in the International Bank for Reconstruction and Development, the International Development Association, the International Finance Corporation [...] and the International Monetary Fund [...] *shall advance the cause of human rights*' (emphasis added).[65] And: 'the Secretary of the Treasury shall instruct each Executive Director of the above institutions to consider in carrying out his duties: (1) specific actions by either the executive branch or the Congress as a whole on individual bilateral assistance programs because of human rights considerations; (2) the extent to which the economic assistance provided by the above institutions directly benefit the needy people in the recipient country.'[66] The law is explicitly reminding US executive directors to take human rights into consideration when taking decisions in the context of IFIs, including the option *not* to take a decision if the programme at hand is not in the interest of addressing and solving the basic needs of people – read: is not in the interest of the realisation of human rights such as the right to food, the right to adequate health care, and the right to housing of the people living in the borrowing States.

From a strictly legal point of view, such laws are not necessary because States and their representatives are already obliged to act in line with their human rights obligations when taking action with external human rights effects.[67] From another perspective, however, there is nothing wrong with making such obligations even more specific. The key question then is whether or not the 'cause' of human rights and the serving of basic human needs will be understood and interpreted in line with existing international human rights law. If the latter is the case, it would make sense for other IFI Member States to follow the US example.

---

65 22 U.S. Code §262d – Human rights and United States assistance policies with international financial institutions, the section on Policy Goals.

66 *Ibidem*, the section on Policy Considerations for Executive Directors of Institutions in Implementation of Duties.

67 See: Fons Coomans and Menno T. Kamminga (eds), *Extraterritorial Application of Human Rights Treaties*, Antwerp/Oxford: Intersentia, 2004, and recently: Malcolm Langford, Wouter Vandenhole, Martin Scheinin and Willem van Genugten (eds), *Global Justice, State Duties. The Extraterritorial Scope of Economic, Social and Cultural Rights in International Law*, Cambridge: Cambridge University Press, 2013, *passim*.

3.6. OBLIGATIONS FOLLOWING FROM (LEGAL) RELATIONSHIPS BETWEEN THE IFIs AND PRIVATE SUBCONTRACTORS

Concluding this part on human rights obligations, a few remarks have to be made on the relationship between the IFIs and private subcontractors. Without discussing here the direct human rights obligations of businesses themselves, one can discern two different relationships between an IFI and its private subcontractors. The first concerns a *direct* link, in the case, for instance, of security guards working for an IFI, but legally employed by a private security company. An *indirect* relationship is created when an IFI supports collaboration between a State and a private subcontractor, for instance, within the context of a public–private partnership.

In situations where there is a *direct* relationship, the IFI is first of all obliged to act as carefully as possible when selecting a subcontractor; for example, by conducting an extensive check of its past performance and by drawing up contracts that contain adequate provisions in case the subcontractor violates norms in the field of human rights law. If human rights are violated by the private contractor, the IFI would at least have a co-obligation to find an adequate solution, in whatever form (compensation, reparation, satisfaction). Human rights obligations and the consequences of the violations thereof cannot be contracted away and, in the end, the interests of the victims of violations of such obligations should not be neglected if, for instance, the private subcontractor goes bankrupt or changes its legal status after (or during) the contract period.[68]

In April 2010, the heads of leading multilateral development banks (MDBs) signed an agreement to cross-debar firms and individuals found to have engaged in wrongdoing in MDB-financed development projects.[69] Under this agreement, entities debarred by one MDB may be sanctioned for the same misconduct in the context of other participating development banks. The goal is to use a list of debarred firms ('black list') to close a

---

68 More on such obligations and related (State) responsibility issues in: Willem van Genugten, Nicola Jägers and Evgeni Moyakine, 'Private Military and Security Companies, Transnational Private Regulation and Public International Law: From the Public to the Private and Back Again?', in: Jernej Letnar Černič and Tara Van Ho (eds), *Human Rights and Business: Direct Corporate Accountability for Human Rights*, Oisterwijk: Wolf Legal Publishers, forthcoming (2015).

69 'Agreement for Mutual Enforcement of Debarment Decisions', 2010. Available at: http://go.worldbank.org/B699B73Q00.

loophole that has previously allowed a firm debarred by one MDB to continue obtaining contracts financed by other MDBs. Although this initiative is primarily situated in the battle against fraud and corruption, its scope can be broadened to include human rights violations.

When confronted with human rights violations in an *indirect* relationship, it is more difficult, but not impossible to establish the exact obligations of the IFI. In this situation it is important to establish to what extent the IFI has control over the subcontractor hired by the borrowing State. As far as the IFI influences the decision over which private actors will be involved, it has an obligation to act as described in the context of the direct relationship. In any event, and in whatever way the decision on hiring the subcontractor is taken, an examination of the factual control relationship between the IFI, the Member State and the private corporation will be called for. This relationship, however, is a matter of attributing conduct rather than of (human rights) obligations per se.

CHAPTER 4

ATTRIBUTING UNLAWFUL CONDUCT TO IFIs AND THEIR MEMBER STATES

Being bound by human rights obligations is one thing, determining the exact responsibility for the violation of such obligations by the IFIs as co-duty-bearers in the domain of international human rights law is something else entirely, and is the logical next step to be discussed. This chapter discusses three aspects of the attribution of responsibility for unlawful conduct: the attribution of unlawful conduct and responsibility to IFIs (subsection 4.1); what it means to be 'in control' (subsection 4.2); and primary, subsidiary and shared responsibility (subsection 4.3).

4.1. ATTRIBUTION AND RESPONSIBILITY

The circumstances under which international organisations may be held responsible for internationally wrongful acts have been laid down in the International Law Commission's *Draft Articles on the Responsibility of International Organizations.*[70] The DARIO rules are used here as one of the possible lenses through which one can look at the (co-)responsibility of IFIs for the violation of human rights obligations. In light of Article 4 of DARIO, two conditions are required under international law for the responsibility of IFIs to be established: firstly, the breach of one of their international obligations, and, secondly, that the breach at issue is attributable to the IFI. As to the latter requirement, the conduct to be attributed will most of the time be the official conduct of the organs and agents of the IFIs acting within the overall framework of their functions, irrespective of the excess of authority or contravention of instructions (see also Article 2(c) and Article 8 DARIO).

The acts and omissions of IFIs may give rise to human rights violations where they aid or assist (Article 14), or direct and control (Article 15) a State (or another international organisation) in the commission of a wrongful act. The International Law Commission Commentary to the

70 An excerpt of the Draft Articles on the Responsibility of International Organizations can be found in Annex II.

Draft Articles[71] focuses especially on two conditions: the *competence* of the international organisation and the *intention* of the Member State. Article 61 of DARIO provides that the organisation must have *competence* in relation to the subject matter of the State's international obligation at hand before it can be held responsible, and the Commentary to the Article makes it clear that these situations are not limited to the transfer of a State's functions to an organisation. It provides:

> What is relevant for international responsibility to arise under the present article, is that the international obligation covers the area in which the international organization is provided with competence. The obligation may specifically relate to that area or be more general, as in the case of obligations under treaties for the protection of human rights.[72]

The DARIO rules, thus, clearly address obligations linked to the international organisations *themselves* and the responsibilities that might be invoked if they fail to meet their obligations. As to the *intention* of Member States, acting in the context of international organisations, it is stated in Article 61 that:

> [A] State member of an international organization incurs international responsibility if, by taking advantage of the fact that the organization has competence in relation to the subject matter of one of the State's international obligations, it circumvents that obligation by causing the organization to commit an act that, if committed by the State, would have constituted a breach of the obligation.

In the case of a Member State acting in the context of an IFI, the attribution of misconduct relates to the obligation the State has as a sovereign State, either because it is a party to a convention the substance of which is at stake in a concrete IFI decision or action, or because the relevant norm has a customary law character. Basically, in relation to such obligations it does not make a difference whether the State acts on its own, or in the context of an IFI. As to the attribution of conduct violating such standards, the basic rule is that where the State is 'in control', it must accept the corresponding

71 Available at: http://legal.un.org/ilc/texts/instruments/english/commentaries/9_11_2011.pdf.

72 Commentary to Article 61 DARIO, para. 6.

responsibility (more on 'in control' in subsection 4.2). The same goes, *mutatis mutandis* for the IFIs themselves.

Although very relevant, it would go too far in the present context to discuss at length the specific responsibilities of both actors in relation to each of the elements of the tripartite human rights typology (respect, protect, fulfil).[73] Instead, this publication focuses on two issues: what does it mean exactly that a State or an IFI is 'in control' and how is responsibility divided between IFIs and Member States?

4.2. 'IN CONTROL'

In subsection 3.3 of this publication mention was made of two of the General Comments of the CESCR relevant to the present context 'reminding' States of what they have to do when acting in the context of international organisations such as the WBG and the IMF. While specifying the required conduct, the CESCR also discussed on several occasions the scope of that 'desired behaviour'. But what can realistically be asked of State parties to the International Covenant on Economic, Social and Cultural Rights when active in the context of international organisations, more specifically IFIs? In some of its Concluding Observations, for instance, in 2001 in reaction to the periodical State report by Germany, the CESCR encouraged 'the State party, as a member of international financial institutions, in particular the IMF and the World Bank, *to do all it can* to ensure that the policies and decisions of those organisations are in conformity with the obligations of States parties to the Covenant' (emphasis added).[74] I consider this to be an interesting formulation, which, however, at the same time is rather vague and far from being outcome-oriented or linked to hard-duty language. Nevertheless, I agree with Magdalena Sepulveda that the words can also be read as a call upon States to perform 'an active role aimed at the

---

73 See extensively: Ashfaq Khalfan and Ian Seiderman, 'Extraterritorial Human Rights Obligations: Wider Implications of the Maastricht Principles and the Continuing Accountability Challenge', in: Wouter Vandenhole (ed.), *Challenging Territoriality in Human Rights Law: Building Blocks for a Plural and Diverse Duty-Bearer Regime*, Routledge, forthcoming (2015).

74 Example taken from M. Langford, F. Coomans and F. Gómez Isa, 'Extraterritorial Duties in International Law', in: Malcolm Langford, Wouter Vandenhole, Martin Scheinin and Willem van Genugten (eds), *supra* n. 67, p. 104.

implementation of the Covenant'.[75] But what is 'active'? Ashfaq Khalfan observes that:

> Requiring that a State 'do all it can' to ensure that international organizations conform to the International Covenant on Economic, Social and Cultural Rights implicitly requires that States have obligations to respect, protect and fulfill ESC rights in the context of their participation within such organizations.[76]

Although Khalfan reads something into the findings of the CESCR, I think he draws the right conclusion from the intention of the Committee, while making that intention more specific than the wording chosen by the Committee itself. However, unless we think that the obligations to respect, protect and fulfil human rights are totally clear in each and every situation – which is not the case, despite numerous legal and semi-legal instruments and extensive case law – one still needs to go a few steps further.

In an attempt to create more clarity on such issues, the Maastricht ETO Principles refer to the obligation to avoid causing harm:

> States must desist from acts and omissions that create *a real risk* of nullifying or impairing the enjoyment of economic, social and cultural rights extraterritorially. The responsibility of States is engaged where such nullification or impairment is a *foreseeable result* of their conduct. *Uncertainty* about potential impacts *does not constitute justification for such conduct.* (Principle 13, emphasis added)

I consider this to be good overall guideline, although applying it in full in the context of IFIs seems to be a nearly impossibly high threshold (more on that below).

Before returning to the responsibility of IFIs specifically, it makes sense to have a look at related standard-setting efforts and outcomes in the relation to the concept of being 'in control'. Apart from the CESCR, several other human rights supervisory bodies, as well as, for instance, the International Court of Justice and a number of International Criminal Tribunals (and researchers reflecting upon their case-law), have developed concepts such as 'effective control', 'overall control', 'decisive influence',

---

75 *Ibidem.*

76 Ashfaq Khalfan, 'Division of Responsibility amongst States', in: Malcolm Langford, Wouter Vandenhole, Martin Scheinin and Willem van Genugten (eds), *supra* n. 67, p. 311.

'due diligence', 'positive obligations', 'sphere of influence', and 'proximity'; when looking at the outcome side rather than the input side, they have come up with notions such as 'equivalent protection', 'conduct doctrine' and the 'effects doctrine'.[77]

The search is for an adequate coining of the scope of human rights obligations of whatever actor and the establishment of the corresponding responsibility for human rights violations if that actor is considered to be 'in control'. In many cases, although not exclusively, these efforts have been undertaken in the context of the violation of civil and political rights, of international humanitarian law, of international criminal law and of 'hard' parts of general international law, such as the duty to respect the territorial integrity of States. It is not always easy to find relevant criteria – cumulatively – in the context of (a) violations of economic, social and cultural rights, (b) taking place extraterritorially, by and through (c) the channels of the IFIs and/or their Member States. In some situations and cases, however, it is not too difficult to develop such criteria – one can think of the construction of a typical World Bank-funded dam leading to the forced eviction of a local indigenous community (the phenomenon also known as 'villagisation'),[78] which would involve a number of violations of human rights, amongst them economic, social and cultural rights, depending on the concrete situation at hand – but such examples are often *too* easy and not able to be applied in less clear situations.

This becomes even more apparent if the nuances of the issue of 'causation of human rights violations' are explicitly added to the spectrum. Under what circumstance can one speak of a sufficient causal link between an activity of an IFI or an IFI Member State and a specific human rights violation, in order to hold that actor responsible for the violation? Even

---

77 See, out of many sources, Smita Narula, 'International Financial Institutions, Transnational Corporations and Duties of States', in: Malcolm Langford, Wouter Vandenhole, Martin Scheinin and Willem van Genugten (eds), *supra* n. 67, *passim*, esp. pp. 120–125 and pp. 140–147; Maarten den Heijer and Rick Lawson, 'Extraterritorial Human Rights and the Concept of "Jurisdiction"', in: *Ibidem*, esp. pp. 172–182; Cedric Ryngaert, 'Jurisdiction: Towards a Reasonableness Test', in: *Ibidem*, *passim*; August Reinisch, 'Aid or Assistance and Direction and Control between States and International Organizations in the Commission of Internationally Wrongful Acts', *International Organizations Law Review*, Vol. 7, 2010, *passim*; Paul De Hert and Fisnik Korenica, 'The Doctrine of Equivalent Protection: Its Life and Legitimacy Before and After the European Union's Accession to the European Convention on Human Rights', *German Law Journal*, Vol. 13, 2012, pp. 874–895.

78 See for instance Human Rights Watch, *supra* n. 42, *passim*.

more difficult is the causal relationship between an omission to act and the failure to prevent serious violations. In some cases one might be able to establish such links – the above-mentioned forced evictions can again serve as a possible example, although even there it depends on the exact facts of the case whether or not the actor might claim the presence of circumstances precluding wrongfulness (see Chapter V, DARS).

Sigrun Skogly has observed how difficult it is to determine causality in the context of extraterritorial human rights obligations. In doing so, she identifies two types of 'hurdles': 'First, the determination of which acts and omissions actually led to outcomes that may be categorised as human rights violations; and, second, the identification of international legal requirements that may make those acts and omissions unlawful.'[79] Taking such key legal issues into account in the context of the work of IFIs, and including the (interplay of) obligations discussed in Chapter 3, it is clear that it is not easy to establish a standard of control that will be workable in each and every situation that IFIs and their Member States are faced with in the context of drafting and executing their policies, programmes and projects.

Regardless of whether or not such an overall, all-embracing standard is in place, case-by-case analyses would be needed to establish the exact level of control and the corresponding responsibilities. I agree with Martin Scheinin, who has observed on several occasions that 'facticity creates normativity', meaning that a 'contextual assessment of the factual circumstances'[80] of a case or a situation should lead the discussion on establishing jurisdiction and the consequences thereof.[81] However, such

---

79 Sigrun Skogly, 'Causality and Extraterritorial Human Rights Obligations', in: Malcolm Langford, Wouter Vandenhole, Martin Scheinin and Willem van Genugten (eds), *supra* n. 67, p. 235.

80 Martin Scheinin, 'Just Another Word? Jurisdiction in the Roadmaps of State Responsibility and Human Rights', in: Malcolm Langford, Wouter Vandenhole, Martin Scheinin and Willem van Genugten (eds), *supra* n. 67, p. 212.

81 It is an approach, practised already in many ways, for instance in a number of Dutch court cases in relation to the (co-)responsibility of the Netherlands for the massacre in Srebrenica in the summer of 1995. In a judgement of 16 July 2014, the district court of The Hague defines 'effective control' as 'factual control', clarifying that effective control is 'actual say over specific actions whereby all of the actual circumstances and the particular context of the case must be examined'. While the Dutch battalion ('Dutchbat') that had to protect the Muslims in Srebrenica against the Serbs acted as part of a UN peacekeeping operation, the court (nevertheless) found the Netherlands responsible for the deaths of 300 Muslim men. The reasoning: Dutchbat was 'in control' as well and had the option

a case-by-case approach does not have to be undertaken without any normative guidance. In the end, it is all about establishing sufficient factual links between the decision and/or action and the (negative) outcomes – which can be done by independent third parties (courts, committees, fact-finding commissions) – leading to justifiable and reasonable outcomes. One can refer here to Cedric Ryngaert's 'reasonableness test', inspired by US tort law.[82]

Combining the perspectives of Skogly, Scheinin and Ryngaert, we are in the domain of analysing and judging concrete situations, inspired as well as steered by the human rights obligations of the actors concerned and by the system of attribution of unlawful conduct as developed in the context of the DARS and DARIO rules, and further specified by key legal and semi-legal organs, endowed with legal and semi-legal authority. If this judging and analysing work is done by independent experts in human rights law, acting in whatever frame (again: courts, committees, fact-finding commissions) and, if relevant, in connection with other disciplines (economics, finance, anthropology), one can trust that, also in the context of the IFIs, progress can be made along the lines discussed in this article.

4.3. PRIMARY, SUBSIDIARY AND SHARED RESPONSIBILITY

As observed, there is a direct link between being 'in control', including the establishment of causal links between decisions/actions and outcomes, and the attribution of conduct violating international human rights law to the actor concerned, as well as the establishment of the corresponding responsibility. The same reasoning can be applied when the IFI and the Member State are acting jointly. They will then (have to) face the consequences of their shared responsibility, established through procedures outlined above and leading to the apportionment of responsibility according to the relative weight of the (non-)acts conducted and the violations caused.

---

to avoid that the Muslim men were handed over to the Serbs, while Dutchbat also 'should have known' that the men were likely to be killed by the Serbs. See: ECLI:NL:RBDHA:2014:8748, judgement of 16 July 2014 of the district court in The Hague. The judgement is subject to appeal.

82 Cedric Ryngaert, 'Jurisdiction: Towards a Reasonableness Test', in: Malcolm Langford, Wouter Vandenhole, Martin Scheinin and Willem van Genugten (eds), *supra* n. 67, esp. p. 198.

The DARIO rules and the Commentary to it make a distinction between the invocation of primary and subsidiary responsibility and of joint and several responsibility. The first is to my mind a matter of dividing responsibility and providing for a backup in case the invocation of the primary responsibility fails; the second relates to what is called 'shared responsibility'. As to the first, the DARIO rules state that '[w]here an international organization and one or more States or other international organizations are responsible for the same internationally wrongful act, the responsibility of each State or organization may be invoked in relation to that act' (Article 48(1)), and that that responsibility 'may be invoked insofar as the invocation of the primary responsibility has not led to reparation' (Article 48(2)). The primary responsibility might either relate to the IFI *or* the Member States, depending on the policy, programme or project at hand. The International Law Commission Commentary adds, as to the corresponding obligation to provide reparation, that there will be cases 'in which a State or an international organization bears only subsidiary responsibility, to the effect that it would have an obligation to provide reparation only if, and to the extent that, the primarily responsible State or international organization fails to do so'.[83] Conceptually speaking, this language is clear.

As to the shared responsibility, the Commentary to the DARIO states, without being very specific, that '[a]cceptance of responsibility by a State could entail either subsidiary responsibility or joint and several responsibility', while adding that 'the same applies to responsibility based on reliance', and that '[as] a general rule, only a rebuttable presumption may be stated'.[84] I agree with Ashfaq Khalfan and Ian Seiderman that 'the principle of joint responsibility does not apply to a State that can show it has taken all reasonable steps to secure human rights in its conduct that has effect beyond borders'.[85] Although this remark relates to the joint responsibility of States acting extraterritorially, the same reasoning can be applied to the responsibilities shared by a State and an IFI. The 'persistent objector', a concept developed in the context of customary international law, but, by analogy, useful in the present context as well, cannot be blamed for the conduct if it has indeed taken all reasonable steps to avoid that conduct.

---

83 Commentary to DARIO, p. 77.

84 *Ibidem*, p. 99.

85 Ashfaq Khalfan and Ian Seiderman, *supra* n. 73 (forthcoming; no page numbers available).

The question then comes up as to whether or not the concepts discussed in subsection 4.2 (on 'in control') are adequate and sufficient to address all attribution aspects of 'shared responsibility'. Measuring the level of control of each actor individually might lead to either an overlap in attributing conduct to each actor or, alternatively, a gap in such attribution. Both actors might also hide behind one another, creating the risk that the victims of such conduct might end up without responsibility (primary, subsidiary or shared) being recognised or adequate measures of reparation made. As pointed out by Wouter Vandenhole, we might then need concepts such as 'complicity'.[86] He observes that in the international domain the term complicity is used in the context of direct human rights obligations of companies ('corporate complicity'), while one can also refer to the domain of international criminal law and concepts such as a 'joint criminal enterprise'. In both contexts these words have a specific meaning, while the application of the layered composition of the concept – for instance: 'direct, indirect and silent complicity', also discussed by Vandenhole – will lead to specific outcomes in whatever new context the concept is applied.

The key point, however, is clear: in case of joint actions violating whatever parts of international human rights law, there is a need for concepts addressing the issue of overlapping and shared responsibilities. And, while authorising the previously mentioned 'independent third bodies' to do the analyses and judging of concrete situations and cases, weighing all this and apportioning responsibility accordingly, again the criteria unfolded in the section 'in control' is relevant. In all cases the bottom line is that, according to present international human rights law, the responsibility for not causing human rights harm, for actively implementing human rights norms according to the leading tripartite typology, and for taking effective remedial measures in case of violations concerns all actors whose activities in fact affect people's lives. A realistic approach to the establishment of the level of control and the corresponding responsibilities, taking into account all the difficulties that IFIs are facing, will unavoidably lead to the acceptance of these responsibilities.

---

86 Wouter Vandenhole, 'Obligations and responsibility in a multiple and diverse duty-bearer human rights regime', in Wouter Vandenhole, *supra* n. 73 (forthcoming). Also see the complexities he discusses when introducing the term in another context than usual.

CHAPTER 5
ACCOUNTABILITY AND REDRESS

In each and every situation that entails the risk, or actual occurrence, of human rights violations, effective accountability mechanisms must be available. These mechanisms have to provide victims or possible victims of such violations with effective judicial or non-judicial means of testing the legality, and practical consequences, of IFI policies, programmes and projects, including the role of IFI Member States, and to have consequences attached to these if so required from a human rights perspective.

This chapter discusses a number of (selected) issues within this domain relevant to further specify what accountability and redress mean for IFIs. The focus is on measuring standards for effective accountability and redress (subsection 5.1); human rights impact assessments (subsection 5.2); existing IFI accountability mechanisms (subsection 5.3); and mediation, arbitration and related dialogue-based ways of conflict resolution (subsection 5.4).

5.1. SUBSTANTIVE AND PROCEDURAL STANDARDS

One can find a range of international instruments reflecting upon accountability and redress in the case of violations of international law, no matter which actor (States, international organisations, companies). In the following, I take the words used in the DARS, DARIO, Maastricht ETO Principles, and UNGPs as inspiration, not because they are legally binding in each and every situation discussed in this chapter, but because they reflect common sense views on the need to provide reparation in the case of internationally wrongful acts, as well as how that could and should be done in practice. The words chosen are presented here in a descriptive, non-problematised way (italics added for emphasis).

The DARS provide that States are responsible for internationally wrongful acts and that they are 'under an obligation: (a) to *cease* that act, if it is continuing; (b) to offer appropriate assurances and guarantees of *non-repetition*, if circumstances so require' (Article 30). Further to that, responsible States are under an obligation 'to make *full reparation* for the injury caused by the internationally wrongful act', while '[i]njury includes any damage, whether *material or moral*, caused by the internationally wrongful act of a State' (Article 31). Further to this, it is stated that the responsible States 'may *not rely on the provisions of its internal law* as justification for failure to comply with its obligations under this part' (Article 32).

Other articles of DARS specify the issue of reparation, which 'shall take the form of *restitution*, *compensation* and *satisfaction*, either singly or in combination' (Article 34). *Restitution* then means 'to re-establish the situation which existed before the wrongful act was committed, provided and to the extent that restitution: (a) is not materially impossible; (b) does not involve a burden out of all proportion to the benefit deriving from restitution instead of compensation' (Article 35). Article 36 provides that *compensation* covers 'any financially assessable damage including loss of profits insofar as it is established', while Article 37 states that *satisfaction* 'may consist in an acknowledgement of the breach, an expression of regret, a formal apology or another appropriate modality' and that it 'shall not be out of proportion to the injury and may not take a form humiliating to the responsible State'.

Some nuances left aside here, the DARIO follow the same line of reasoning. In Article 33, on the 'Scope of international obligations [to repair]', they add that '[t]he obligations of the responsible international organization [...] may be owed to *one or more States*, to one or more other organizations, or to *the international community as a whole*, depending in particular on the character and content of the international obligation and on the circumstances of the breach'. Articles 34 to 37 elaborate on 'forms of reparation' (again: restitution, compensation and satisfaction).

The Maastricht ETO Principles add in Principles 36 to 38, under the heading 'Accountability and remedies' that 'States must ensure the availability of *effective mechanisms* to provide for accountability in the discharge of their *extraterritorial obligations*' (Principle 36). While specifying this general obligation, the Principles refer to 'systems and procedures for the *full and thorough monitoring of compliance* with their human rights obligations, including through national human rights institutions' (*ibidem*), to 'the right to a *prompt, accessible and effective remedy before an independent authority*' (Principle 37), and to the obligation to ensure that 'remedies are available for *groups as well as individuals*', as well as to the obligation to realise '*victims' participation* in the determination of appropriate remedies' (*ibidem*).

The Maastricht ETO Principles further specify the issue of the *effectiveness of remedies*: '[c]apable of leading to a prompt, thorough and impartial investigation; cessation of the violation if it is ongoing; and adequate reparation, including, as necessary, restitution, compensation, satisfaction, rehabilitation and guarantees of non-repetition' (Principle 37) and, importantly, provide that '[v]ictims have *the right to truth* about the facts and circumstances surrounding the violations, which should *also* be *disclosed to the public*, provided that it causes no further harm to the victim' (Principle 38).

The UNGPs provide for similar views on the duty of States (and businesses) to have mechanisms in place that guarantee *access to effective remedies* in case of human rights violations. They state that '[a]ccess to effective remedy has both *procedural and substantive* aspects', and that the remedies provided by the grievance mechanisms 'may take a *range of substantive forms* the aim of which, generally speaking, will be to counteract or make good any human rights harms that have occurred' (Commentary to UNGP 25). According to the UNGPs, remedies may include '*apologies, restitution, rehabilitation, financial or non-financial compensation* and *punitive sanctions* (whether criminal or administrative, such as fines), as well as the *prevention* of harm through, for example, injunctions or guarantees of *non-repetition*', while procedures for the provision of remedy 'should be *impartial*, protected from *corruption* and *free from political or other attempts to influence the outcome*' (*ibidem*). Interestingly, the Commentary to the UNGPs also reflects upon the term '*grievance*' itself:

> For the purpose of these Guiding Principles, a grievance is understood to be a perceived injustice evoking an individual's or a group's sense of entitlement, which may be based on law, contract, explicit or implicit promises, customary practice, or general notions of fairness of aggrieved communities. The term grievance mechanism is used to indicate any routinized, State-based or non-State-based, judicial or non-judicial process through which grievances concerning business-related human rights abuse can be raised and remedy can be sought (*ibidem*).

Further to that, the UNGPs reflect, in Operational Principle 31, on *effectiveness criteria for non-judicial grievance mechanisms*:

> In order to ensure their effectiveness, non-judicial grievance mechanisms, both State-based and non-State-based, should be:
>
> (a) Legitimate: enabling trust from the stakeholder groups for whose use they are intended, and being accountable for the fair conduct of grievance processes;
> (b) Accessible: being known to all stakeholder groups for whose use they are intended, and providing adequate assistance for those who may face particular barriers to access;

(c) Predictable: providing a clear and known procedure with an indicative time frame for each stage, and clarity on the types of process and outcome available and means of monitoring implementation;
(d) Equitable: seeking to ensure that aggrieved parties have reasonable access to sources of information, advice and expertise necessary to engage in a grievance process on fair, informed and respectful terms;
(e) Transparent: keeping parties to a grievance informed about its progress, and providing sufficient information about the mechanism's performance to build confidence in its effectiveness and meet any public interest at stake;
(f) Rights-compatible: ensuring that outcomes and remedies accord with internationally recognized human rights;
(g) A source of continuous learning: drawing on relevant measures to identify lessons for improving the mechanism and preventing future grievances and harms;

Operational-level mechanisms should also be:

(h) Based on engagement and dialogue: consulting the stakeholder groups for whose use they are intended on their design and performance, and focusing on dialogue as the means to address and resolve grievances.

Summarising the overlapping points, the four documents provide for the following elements, either explicitly or implicitly: starting from the perspective of the victims, including their right to the truth and the right to actively participate in the determination of appropriate remedies, and moving on to the actor (State, company), which has an obligation to prevent possible violations; stop ongoing violations; offer thorough and impartial investigations of the facts; provide for appropriate and effective judicial and/or non-judicial remedies; let these mechanisms be conducted by independent and impartial authorities; take care of prompt and full reparation for material and/or moral damage; and avoid repetition in the future. And all this is to be done in conformity with internationally-accepted procedural and substantive human rights standards ('human rights compatibility').

These formulations can be seen as a non-contested, normative reference framework for the purposes of the present publication. Before proceeding, however, some reflections are needed. First, the documents discussed above underline, either literally or by implication, that in all States effective judicial and non-judicial remedy mechanisms must be available. This might sound self-evident, but does not match the reality in many States worldwide: the word 'must' reflects the setting a 'standard of (absolute) achievement' (see also the Preamble of the Universal Declaration of Human Rights). 'Effectiveness', therefore, first and foremost implies that mechanisms are available and, next to that, that they are applied in a way that actually contributes to the fight for, and guarantee of, 'real accountability', meaning that the mechanisms that are available indeed ensure that compliance with the applicable standards is not only monitored, but that the outcomes are also enforced.

A second issue to be underlined is the issue of 'preventing harms from compounding and grievances from escalating', as the Commentary to UNGP 29 states. While many international instruments do focus on *ex post* reparation for wrongful acts, despite a spread of references to preventing harm as well, the focus on prevention should lead. If human rights violations nevertheless (tend to) occur, it is mandatory to my mind to have, at a minimum, 'early warning' mechanisms in place, showing sensitivity for the problems at stake and ensuring that 'small problems don't become big ones'. Such mechanisms can be situated between prevention and reparation, and, depending on the situation, are ideally closer to the first than to the last on this continuum.

Thirdly, 'effectiveness' is often linked to the human rights compatibility of the outcomes of procedures and of the procedures themselves. However, acting in conformity with human rights standards is often not an unambiguous yes or no, but rather a 'more than less'. This element brings in notions of history, learning capacity, 'moving in the right direction', obligations for results and conduct, and, in connection with this, the measurement of progress. It is often stated that there are differences in that respect between civil and political rights and economic, social and cultural rights. In relation to the latter, the following reference to the well-known Article 2(1) of the International Covenant on Economic, Social and Cultural Rights is relevant: State parties promise to use the 'maximum of [their] available resources, *with a view to achieving progressively the full realization of the rights* recognized in the present Covenant' (emphasis added). However, it can be observed that the realisation of many civil and political rights often takes time as well and can also have an evolutionary character. One can think of building up an independent judiciary, with the inclusion of a provision in a constitution as one point of reference and the daily reality as another, totally different, marker of that evolutionary approach. An example of such evolution is the Netherlands, which called itself from the very start a Kingdom (in 1813), a '(liberal) democracy' and 'a rule of law State', despite the fact that female citizens could not vote until over a century later (1919).

Fourthly, the notion of 'human rights compatibility' is key for States and international organisations, as well as the businesses contracted by them; however, given the number of human rights instruments, no-one can ever fully live up to *all* globally-adopted human instruments. Currently, the UN works with a catalogue of 17 'Core International Human Rights Instruments' and more than 90 other 'Universal Human Rights Instruments', varying from a Declaration on the Rights of Mentally Retarded Persons to the Statute of the International Criminal Court. Apart from that, at the international level, a nearly endless amount of (even) soft(er) human rights instruments exist, as well as a range of regional human rights instruments. Against that background, it might be important and realistic in the context of IFIs and human rights to initially apply a specific, somewhat restricted view of 'human rights compatibility'. This idea is well addressed in the *Guidance Tool on Rights-Compatible Grievance Mechanisms*, developed by the Corporate Social Responsibility Initiative of the Harvard Kennedy School of Government.[87] This tool states that human rights-compatible mechanisms need, first of all, to be 'based on such principles as non-discrimination, equity, accountability, empowerment and participation', and 'that processes affecting the lives, well-being and dignity of individuals and groups in question [should be] fundamentally fair and rest on such principles, as inclusion, participation, empowerment, transparency and attention to vulnerable people'.[88] Formulating it in this way, the notion of human rights compatibility is brought back to its fundamental bare essence, while specific human rights violations can be addressed on a case-by-case basis, thus avoiding sticking to core principles in the domain of human rights 'only'.

Furthermore, and maybe needless to add, whether or not – and, if yes, to what extent – such violations take place should be determined by the mechanisms implemented by the previously mentioned independent and impartial authorities. These mechanisms can have many forms, from national and international courts of law to ombudsmen, from OECD National Contact Points to national human rights institutions, from

---

87 John F. Kennedy School of Government, Cambridge MA, *Rights-Compatible Grievance Mechanisms: A Guidance Tool for Companies and Their Stakeholders*, Corporate Social Responsibility Initiative Working Paper No. 41, Cambridge MA: Harvard University, January 2008, available at: www.shiftproject.org/publication/rights-compatible-grievance-mechanisms-guidance-tool-companies-and-their-stakeholders.

88 *Ibidem*, p. 2 and p. 7 respectively.

mediation, conciliation and arbitration to other national or international procedures or instruments that might entail effective ways of addressing the human problems at stake. What follows is a reflection on a number of relevant issues including, to begin, with the issue of how to establish the risk of human rights violation, especially *ex ante*.

5.2. HUMAN RIGHTS IMPACT ASSESSMENT

According to Maastricht ETO Principle 14, 'States must conduct prior assessment, with public participation, of the risks and potential extraterritorial impacts of their laws, policies and practices on the enjoyment of economic, social and cultural rights', while '[t]he assessment must [...] be undertaken to inform the measures that States must adopt to prevent violations or ensure their cessation as well as to ensure effective remedies'. Although the Maastricht ETO Principles relate only to economic, social and cultural rights, this principle would equally apply to civil and political rights, and, on the actor side, to States while acting as members of IFIs and to the IFIs themselves. Despite progress within and around existing accountability mechanisms – to be discussed in subsection 5.3 – there is continuing resistance from IFIs, albeit from the IMF more than from the World Bank, to integrate 'human rights checks' into their operations more progressively. This resistance includes to human rights impact assessments (HRIAs), particularly *ex ante* assessments, into the decision-making processes for individual projects, country strategies and, ultimately, loan design and dispersal.

The original 2003 Tilburg Guiding Principles called for HRIAs to be conducted at a time when both the conceptualisation and the practise of such assessments were still in their infancy. More than a decade ago, in contrast to the relative establishment and acceptance of environmental and social impact assessment at that time, no widely-known HRIA had been undertaken. There was extensive disagreement, even in the human rights community, about what a HRIA was and what it entailed, and the earliest of the influential methodologies in the field had only just been developed. Now, however, general principles on such assessments have been settled and detailed methodologies developed.[89]

---

89 See for instance Siobhán McInerney-Lankford and Hans-Otto Sano, *Human Rights Indicators in Development*, Washington: World Bank & the Nordic Trust Fund,

It is now generally agreed that a HRIA would entail: the explicit utilisation of the human rights legal framework; independent assessors; a transparent process of assessment, as to the information on which it is based and the options for public submissions; participation by all stakeholders, with particular attention to the voice of affected communities; the inclusion of relevant expertise, human rights experts being in the lead, but including experts from other fields (such as finance, economics, trade, and investment) as necessary; and adequate funding of the assessment in order to ensure high quality and legitimacy, as well as the accuracy and sufficiency of data. Further to this criteria, assessments should regularly include a *preliminary study* to establish which human rights and which populations and communities are potentially affected by any given decision or actual activity. This 'screening' is intended to inform the decision as to whether an assessment is warranted or not, and to make the exercise feasible and focused. The assessors should determine the details of the process relevant to the rights and populations identified at the screening stage. These details would include identifying the appropriate persons, groups, bodies and communities to consult; the appropriate human rights indicators to use; and the specific methodology of the assessment itself. Most importantly, *the assessment itself* should focus on the equity of impacts, negative or positive, across groups, communities and sections of society and should lead to manageable and implementable conclusions and recommendations, allowing evaluation mechanisms to see to it that the conclusions and recommendations are implemented, including the provision of an avenue for stakeholder complaints should there be insufficient weight given to the assessment.

Saying that, the HRIAs must be 'integrated' into the decision-making processes within both the IMF and WBG means that the recommendations and conclusions of HRIAs should not be simply 'factored into' the decisions as one among a number of other competing and more familiar factors, such as mainstream economic and financial analysis, as a box-ticking process, and then disregarded in favour of these more established viewpoints. While acknowledging that human rights are by no means the only concern in decision-making by IFIs, a human rights analysis should be viewed by IFIs as necessary prior to the decision-making process and integral to the

2010; Nordic Trust Fund, *Study on Human Rights Impact Assessments; A Review of the Literature, Differences with other Forms of Assessments and Relevance for Development*, February 2013.

creation and selection of options. It can be easily observed that human rights will not give detailed answers to every aspect of decisions, nor do they need to. However, they can, and regularly will, help set a boundary and create a certain space within which economic rationalism can operate, as well as a space in which trade-offs can be made. In this respect, mention can be made of the Nordic Trust Fund, operating out of the Operations Policy and Country Services division of the World Bank. This Fund was formed in 2006 as 'a knowledge and learning initiative to help the World Bank develop a more informed view on human rights'.[90] HRIAs are in one way or another indispensable to the development of such an informed view.

5.3. EXISTING IFI ACCOUNTABILITY MECHANISMS

The willingness to operate in a transparent way, while including participation by the people who will be affected by the concerned decisions and actions, is generally seen as a prerequisite for the prevention of human rights violations or for effective remedying of harm caused through judicial or non-judicial mechanisms in the case of actual violations. Both the IMF and WBG have been working on transparency and participation issues in the recent past, also in the context of mechanisms already set in place. The Safeguard Policies of the World Bank, for instance, constitute an example of a self-regulatory mechanism binding on its staff, which includes areas with a clear human rights dimension, such as involuntary resettlement, indigenous peoples and the environment, and an increasing emphasis on the participation of stakeholders in policy-making processes. In addition, the transparency arrangements of the Bank were enhanced in 2010, with the adoption of the broad Access to Information Policy, whereby information about projects under preparation and implementation, analytic and advisory activities, and Board proceedings are to be made accessible to the public.[91]

As to the IMF, it can be observed that transparency in decision-making has also been strengthened over the last decade through the adoption of a transparency policy by the Executive Board, mandating an increased

90 *Ibidem*, back side.

91 See: http://web.worldbank.org/WBSITE/EXTERNAL/PROJECTANDOPERATIONS/EXTINFODISCLOSURE/0,,menuPK:64864911~pagePK:4749265~piPK:4749256~theSitePK:5033734,00.html.

liberalisation of its document disclosure policy. Staff papers prepared for Board consideration and Executive Board minutes are now made public, as well as the IMF's views and analysis of economic developments and policies in a specific country through the issuing of Public Information Notices (PINs). Moreover, communication channels between the Executive Directors and the media, civil society organisations and the academic community have been significantly strengthened.[92]

As a step away from transparency towards actual supervision, the World Bank Inspection Panel, established in 1993, has held that the Bank is responsible for putting into place adequate legal covenants in project documents to ensure that all relevant policy requirements will be met; to advise the borrower; to ensure policy compliance; and, in the case of project implementation, to take the necessary steps required by the Bank's policy on supervision of it projects and programmes. The extent to which the Bank is adequately supervising projects during implementation and responding to issues of policy compliance as they arise is a recurring and major element in a number of Inspection Panel investigations. Affected parties can challenge any act or omission of the Bank as a result of its failure to follow set policies and procedures before the World Bank Inspection Panel, provided that such failure has had, or threatens to have, a material adverse effect. However, it should be noted that the Inspection Panel's mandate is strictly limited to the existing operational policies and procedures of the World Bank, which means that to address human rights violations the aggrieved must largely rely on the safeguard policies and performance standards as adopted.[93] Although the Inspection Panel is not competent to establish human rights violations, it does allow for an (internal) assessment of the World Bank's compliance with its operational policies and procedures. The next step, following from the Bank's own position-taking on human rights issues, could be to include explicitly in the Inspection Panel's mandate the competence to look at human rights violations linked to World Bank programmes and projects *per se*, including the option for affect parties to lodge complaints about human rights related issues.

In addition to the Inspection Panel, the Office of the Compliance Advisor/Ombudsman (CAO), established in 1999 as an independent recourse mechanism for projects supported by the International Finance

92 See recently: *Review of the IMF's Communications Strategy*, 8 August 2014, available at: www.imf.org/external/np/pp/eng/2014/063014.pdf.

93 See Adam McBeth, *supra* n. 55, p. 1147 in conjunction with p. 1146.

Corporation and the Multilateral Investment Guarantee Agency (MIGA) (*i.e.* the private sector lending arms of the World Bank Group) works to address, *inter alia*, the concerns of individuals or communities affected by IFC/MIGA projects. The CAO responds to complaints from project-affected communities with the goal of enhancing especially social and environmental outcomes on the ground. The mandate of the CAO, which works on the basis of mediation and mediation-related procedures, is rather flexible and the Office may take human rights related issues on board if presented as relevant by the conflicting parties. Adam McBeth calls this a 'relatively holistic approach', allowing for more space because the CAOs mandate 'is not limited to the proper application of World Bank policies, unlike the Inspection Panel', and can thus avoid the frustration the Panel is sometimes confronted with on formal grounds.[94] In addition, importantly, the CAO is based 'on the desire to resolve disputes rather than apportion blame' (more on that below in subsection 5.4).[95]

The IMF's Independent Evaluation Office (IEO), established in 2001, focuses on providing independent evaluations of IMF policies, governance and activities and on making recommendations to the Executive Board for remedial action or the revision of the organisation's structure and operational policies. While the IEO's mandate allows for flexibility in the possible evaluation topics and consultations with informed and interested parties outside the IMF, affected or interested parties cannot challenge IMF programmes and policies. As McBeth observes, 'the IEO rather than the complainant holds the ability to initiate the process' and 'the intended outcome of the evaluation is advice to IMF management as part of "institutional learning"' rather than 'resolution of complaints or rectification of wrongs suffered by a particular person or group'.[96]

5.4. ARBITRATION, MEDIATION AND DIALOGUE-BASED CONFLICT RESOLUTION

It is beyond the scope of the present publication to present and discuss all national and international options for dealing with the human rights consequences of the policies, programmes and projects of the WBG and the

94 *Ibidem*, p. 1150.
95 *Ibidem*, p. 1151.
96 *Ibidem*, p. 1153.

IMF. Mention has already been made of, for instance, the UN Committee on Economic, Social and Cultural Rights and its view of what Member States of these two (and other) IFIs should do. Apart from human rights supervisory bodies, other 'general' supervisory or dispute settlement bodies can be of importance, such as the Permanent Court of Arbitration (PCA), established by treaty in 1899. Although the PCA was originally established for inter-State arbitration, now other actors may also bring disputes before the PCA, *e.g.* a State and an international organisation; two or more international organisations; a State and a private party; and an international organisation and a private party. However, the jurisdiction of this arbitral tribunal is established through an agreement between the involved parties. This means that, although the procedures of the PCA might allow access as such, the dispute will only be accepted if there is an agreement between the parties involved (including the WBG and the IMF) to accept the jurisdiction of the PCA. It is argued that the WBG and IMF should commit themselves to fully accepting the jurisdiction of the PCA in disputes in which they are involved.

The possible benefits of arbitration, using the procedures under the PCA or not, are manifold. Arbitration can often produce a result more speedily than judicial proceedings. Furthermore, arbitration allows the parties to a conflict great freedom in selecting the adjudicators. In the case of direct or indirect human rights violations by an IFI, the choice of arbitrator can ensure that at least one arbitrator is familiar with the interests of the financial institution, while another arbitrator can be selected because of his/her significant human rights expertise. Disadvantages of arbitration, however, are that the procedure can be confidential if one party or both parties so require, and, for instance, that the parties not only pay the cost of preparing their own cases, but also the fees of the arbitrators and other costs involved.

The focus of *any* conflict resolution mechanism in which IFIs or their Member States are involved should be on the effectiveness of the outcomes, as seen from the perspective of possible victims (individuals and communities), while taking into account the legitimate interests of both IFIs and their Member States. Mediation-based mechanisms might also provide good options, because, when used in an effective manner, they often serve as more efficient, immediate and low-cost dispute resolution instruments than their State-based counterparts. Furthermore, it is crucial to note that, particularly in developing countries, the reliance on national authorities and local institutions often does not allow for the adequate protection of local communities and the restitution of their rights and interests. There are many reasons for this, amongst them a lack of political will to constrain economic and financial actors. Good mediation can accommodate different views and interests, not only those of the parties to a dispute, but also, if relevant, those of the community(s) at large. Further to that, mediation-based mechanisms are more able to look past the irritations and differences that are normal between disputing parties. They can also help to equalise any perceived power imbalances amongst stakeholders; engender trust amongst parties that may be reluctant to participate; garner agreement on a constructive approach for the prevention of similar problems in the future; and make IFIs respond appropriately, even where non-judicial settlement efforts do not lead to a solution to the case at hand.[97] The previously mentioned Office of the Compliance Advisor/Ombudsman has already dealt with a large number of cases. In one of these it observed as follows:

> The CAO recognizes that differences among community members and between communities and the company/sponsor are natural in a mining project on the scale of the proposed [...] project. When these differences are handled wisely and in a good way, the whole community can benefit. To a certain extent, it is to be expected that some tensions and differences will be ongoing and unforeseen problems will arise. Therefore, in addition to trying to solve the immediate complaint issues quickly and effectively, the CAO would encourage local community members and [the company] to discuss and agree on a constructive approach for preventing and dealing with problems and conflicts when they arise in the future – how to raise concerns and how to listen to each other over the long-term so that they can continue to interact and work together even when they disagree [...].[98]

From this quote many general lessons can be drawn. While formulating the problem at hand, in this case relating to a private mining company active in North Maluku, Indonesia, which caused identifiable harm to the local population, the CAO often contextualises the problem, while also linking its approach to issues such as future prevention, including the

97 See Willem van Genugten, Mariya Gromilova, Nicola Jägers, Evgeni Moyakine, and Laura de Vries, *Company-community Conflicts: The Effectiveness of Outcomes of Non-judicial Conflict Resolution. An Exploratory Report*, report prepared for ACCESS Facility, The Hague, October 2013, pp. 52–53.

98 CAO Ombudsman Assessment Report: Complaint Regarding the MIGA PT Weda Bay Nickel Project (#8113), Halmahera Island, North Maluku, Indonesia, quoted in *ibidem*, p. 26.

empowerment of possible future victims. Such approaches engender and sustain communication and build mutual trust, instead of sharpening differences. In contrast, judicial decision-making can polarise parties to a dispute, as they are framed as adversaries, rather than seeking a consensus-based solution that might be in the interests of all parties to the conflict.

However, judicial and related fallback mechanisms always have to be in place as a failsafe to ensure an adequate remedy for human rights violations. At present, this is often not the case. In addition, governments are generally needed to secure outcomes, especially those that are meant to have long-term effects and that might require new legislation or, for instance, protective measures that, in the context of IFC/MIGA projects, cannot be provided by companies alone.

In all cases and at all stages, and whatever conflict resolution mechanisms are used, it is of key importance that people(s) have the right to be adequately informed and to not be excluded from decision-making on matters that affect them. This raises the issue of 'free, prior and informed consent', widely recognised in the context of indigenous peoples[99] and highly relevant in relation to the policies, programmes and projects undertaken by the World Bank Group and the IMF. On a normative level, both IFIs are required, based on existing human rights law, to ensure that the people who are affected by their activities are given the opportunity to participate actively in the decision-making processes that affect them. On a practical level, this participation should be further facilitated in the light of developing applicable international human rights standards and should, again, take into account especially marginalised groups and peoples, including indigenous peoples. In order to implement these standards, the WBG and the IMF should also support initiatives in which co-operation between human rights NGOs and development NGOs is strengthened in order to maximise their effective engagement with IFIs and the communities affected by WBG- and IMF-funded activities. Such initiatives would enable both IFIs to ensure the development of policies, programmes and projects that are consistent with the rights and needs of these communities and that the outcomes are actually accounted for.

Empowerment and capacity building, assisted by human rights and development NGOs where relevant, are important elements in effective and proactive dispute settlement. More importantly, they also contribute to the

99 See recently: S.J. Rombouts, *Having a Say: Indigenous Peoples, International Law and Free, Prior and Informed Consent*, Oisterwijk: Wolf Legal Publishers, 2014.

development of prevention strategies to address possible conflicts at an early stage and foster the capability of communities to solve their own problems in the future, perhaps without third-party intervention. Whether it is a needs assessment at the beginning or participation in the monitoring of the follow up at the end, it all adds to ownership of the problem as well as to (feelings of) recognition and understanding of local habits and views and, thus, most likely, also to local capacity and willingness to implement the outcomes reached in a sustainable manner. In this way, local processes and mechanisms for resolving conflict are strengthened, rather than replaced by processes and mechanisms that might be seen by local communities as alien and inappropriate.

Conflict resolution is not a zero-sum game (a situation in which the gains or losses of one party are the full equivalent of the gains or losses of the other party). This is even more the case in relation to non-judicial conflict resolution. In the end, it is often a matter of degree and balancing. The legitimacy and effectiveness of outcomes then depends on, *inter alia*, to what extent the outcomes are in line with the substantive normative frames used (the 'human rights compatibility'); whether or not the interests at stake have received adequate attention; whether or not the procedures used have been (needless) expensive or time absorbing; whether or not the actual reward (compensation, etc.) is satisfactory; and whether or not measures will be taken that help avoid similar human rights abuses in the future. All of these elements can be qualified as, by-and-large, objective elements, while subjective elements are also key, such as: do people experience the outcome as just? Here, process issues such as transparency and space for participation come into play and community leaders can play a role in convincing people that the outcome is reasonable, despite any higher aims at the beginning of the dispute settlement process. This goes for judicial as well non-judicial dispute settlement, but in the end the non-judicial way of thinking might be much more conducive to this than its judicial counterpart. Again, if a non-judicial dispute resolution mechanism fails, there should be an effective judicial fallback mechanism, either national or international.

CHAPTER 6
CONCLUDING REMARKS

Over the last two decades, many commentaries have been released on the way the WBG and IMF have taken human rights obligations on board, or refrained from doing so. This publication could have set the strict legal obligations and corresponding responsibilities for both IFIs higher, for instance, by presenting more extensive interpretations of already existing case law or by extrapolating trends in the human rights field more progressively than I have done. However, I believe that to do so would have overstretched the legal validity and applicability of developments in the field of international human rights law to IFIs such as the WBG and IMF. Overall, there is a lot of pressure on both organisations, as well as on other multilateral development banks not discussed here, to accept more accountability under international human rights standards. It has been made clear by what standards they are already bound, given the status of international human rights law in 2014, while, as to the extent to which both IFIs, be it to different degrees, still argue that they are *not* bound by such standards, it has been shown that the space for such a position is becoming more and more limited.

It helps to underscore that both IFI are independently moving in a direction in which the relevance of human rights to the fulfilment of their mandates is recognised, be it in the form of small steps following other small steps. In addition, it should not be forgotten that the pronouncements on human rights by both IFIs are only partly relevant from a strictly legal perspective. However, human rights law is best understood as living law and actors such as IFIs can be best considered non-static entities, even given their sometimes static approaches to their own mandates. Both IFIs have entered the human rights doorway, be it to different degrees. And should they want to move backwards or reconsider their respective ways forward, international human rights law as it presently stands can serve as an invitation, but also as a stop sign.

Building on human rights law as 'living law' and seeing both the WBG and IMF as 'non-static entities', it makes sense to put the findings of this publication in a somewhat historical perspective. In relation to that, I would like to refer to a report on the realisation of economic, social and cultural rights, presented a bit more than twenty years ago (in 1992) by the then UN Special Rapporteur on the Realization of Economic, Social and Cultural

Rights, Danilo Türk. He was quite critical of the World Bank's and IMF's structural adjustment programmes and stated that, despite the more recent visions of adjustment by the IMF and World Bank, these programmes still appeared 'far too often to be inspired by economic theory rather than practical experience of the human, political, social and economic impact adjustment had [upon the populations of] more than 70 countries'.[100] He qualified this as 'bitter medicine', his own 'medicine' containing the recommendation 'to integrate human rights yardsticks into any equation measuring the levels of achievement of adjustment programmes'.[101] His line of thinking is clear, his terminology reflecting an approach to the issue of IFIs and human rights that was typical in his day and for international human rights law as it was by then. The long journey towards strengthening the legal character of especially economic, social and cultural rights was only at its very beginning, let alone the extension of human rights law to entities other than States, such as IFIs.

Some economists may argue that the arguments brought forward in this publication and in the Guiding Principles contained in Annex I conflict with certain economic goals. In their eyes, human rights might be an inappropriate field to be incorporated into IFI policies, programmes and projects, because these should be guided by 'sound' economic principles, analysis and expertise. However, the fact that certain economic viewpoints may clash with human rights priorities and the notion that some supposedly necessary economically-informed trade-offs will not fit within the space framed by the human rights obligations of both IFIs and their Member States, are *not* necessarily an indication of an *irreconcilable* conflict between the fields of economics and human rights. Today economists strongly influence politicians acting in the context of the IFIs, partly barring them from adopting value systems that are inspired by disciplines other than mainstream economics. Nevertheless, the awareness of the limitations of exclusively mainstream economic approaches is growing within IFIs. This gradually changing attitude towards the relevance of human rights to their mandates – in the context of the World Bank Group more than in the context of the IMF – can assist both of them in moving forward from their (former) institutionalised preoccupation with a narrow set of economic and financial principles into an internalised appreciation of economic theories that are increasingly amenable to the realisation of human rights goals in the countries in which they operate.

---

100 UN Document E/CN.4/Sub.2/1992/16, 3 July 1992, p. 14.

101 *Ibidem*, p. 18.

ANNEX I

TILBURG-GLOTHRO GUIDING PRINCIPLES ON THE WORLD BANK GROUP, THE INTERNATIONAL MONETARY FUND AND HUMAN RIGHTS

PREAMBLE

- *Recalling* the 2003 Tilburg Guiding Principles on World Bank, IMF and Human Rights, drafted by a group of experts, meeting at Tilburg University, The Netherlands, in October 2001 and April 2002 ('2003 Tilburg Guiding Principles');
- *Considering* the significant overlap between substantive areas covered by international human rights law and the work of the World Bank Group (WBG) and the International Monetary Fund (IMF) on, *inter alia*, improving poor people's access to work, health, education, food and water; promoting the participation of indigenous peoples in decision-making; holding state governments accountable to those under their jurisdiction; and supporting justice reforms;
- *Recalling* that creating the conditions for the realization of human rights is a central goal of human development and a responsibility of all States under, *inter alia*, the Universal Declaration of Human Rights;
- *Reaffirming* the WBGs and IMFs own policy statements, recognizing, albeit in different ways, the growing need to address human rights in a more explicit fashion;
- *Emphasizing* the self-proclaimed role of the WBG and the IMF to support their Member States in fulfilling their human rights obligations while carrying out the policies, projects and programs of both international financial institutions (IFIs);
- *Reviewing* the human rights obligations and responsibilities of the WBG and the IMF in light of developments in the domain of international human rights law over the last decade.

The drafters of the 2014 *Tilburg-GLOTHRO Guiding Principles on the World Bank Group, the International Monetary Fund and Human Rights* have further developed and reformulated the 2003 Tilburg Guiding Principles.

1. LEGAL OBLIGATIONS

- *Guiding Principle 1*: **General International Law Obligations**
  International organizations do have international legal personality, which comes with obligations in the field of international (human rights) law. More specifically, the WBG and the IMF, having entered into Relationship Agreements with the United Nations in accordance with UN Charter Articles 57 and 63, are bound by the UN Charter, customary international law and general principles of law.

- *Guiding Principle 2*: **The 'Political Prohibition'**
  The 'Political Prohibition', conceptually linking activities of the WBG to non-interference into 'the domestic affairs of sovereign States', must be re-interpreted in conformity to modern international human rights law, and applied accordingly.

- *Guiding Principle 3*: **Scope of Human Rights Obligations**
  As institutional subjects and duty-bearers under international law, the WBG and the IMF, and other IFIs accordingly, have the legal obligation to respect, protect and fulfil the realization of all human rights within the scope of their competences and their activities. To this end, the WBG Group and the IMF shall undertake to:

  a) endorse human rights instruments, and accede to those human rights treaties they can formally accede to;
  b) live up to existing international and regional human rights law, including authoritative interpretations thereof by their supervisory bodies;
  c) ensure that the prevention of human rights violations is given priority in the development and actual implementation of their policies, projects and programs;
  d) protect and actively promote human rights within all aspects of their internal functioning;
  e) observe the good governance principle of non-discriminatory participation, through ensuring transparency and accountability in the design and implementation of their policies, projects and programs;
  f) provide adequate reparation for harm in the domain of human rights caused by their activities;
  g) respect the human rights obligations of their Member States.

- *Guiding Principle 4*: **Human Rights Due Diligence**
  The WBG and the IMF have a duty of due diligence to the preparation and execution of their policies, projects and programs to prevent human rights violations, to identify and assess actual and potential human rights impacts, to act upon the findings, to track responses, and to communicate how impacts are

addressed, and shall see human rights due diligence as not a one-off activity but as an ongoing process.

- *Guiding Principle 5*: **Policy Space and Agreements with States**
  Agreements with Member States and borrowing States shall not impede these States from honouring their human rights obligations, nor force them to agree to measures depriving individuals or communities of their rights under domestic or international human rights law.

- *Guiding Principle 6*: **Human Rights Obligations of Member States**
  Member States of the WBG and the IMF, bearing responsibility for determining the policies, projects and programs of the two IFIs, shall act in accordance with their States' international human rights obligations, including their extraterritorial obligations.

- *Guiding Principle 7*: **Obligations of Executive Directors**
  The WBG and the IMF Member States shall take the necessary measures to ensure that the Executive Directors comply with the human rights obligations of the (multiple) States they represent.

- *Guiding Principle 8*: **Partnerships with Other Organizations**
  When entering into partnerships with other organizations, the WBG and the IMF shall consider establishing links to the goals and instruments of such partner organizations, including those within the UN system, and shall determine how these organizations relate to the WBGs and the IMFs policy orientations and decision-making processes, including explicit references to appropriate human rights obligations and objectives.

- *Guiding Principle 9*: **Contracts with Private Business Enterprises**
  When concluding contracts with private business enterprises, the WBG and the IMF shall ensure that those enterprises comply with international human rights standards, regarding projects and programs that entail the risk of human rights violations, enumerating such standards and including specific obligations and responsibilities in relation to the States where the enterprises will be active.

2. RESPONSIBILITY

- *Guiding Principle 10*: **Attribution of Conduct and Corresponding Responsibility to the IFIs**
  The WBG and the IMF shall be held responsible when conduct – be it action or omission – a) is performed in an area where they are factually in control, b)

leads to the non-prevention or actual occurrence of breaches of international human rights law, and c) is attributable to either of them under the law on the responsibility of international organizations, while providing that d) a causal link between the act/omission and the actual violation can be reasonably established by independent third bodies and that e) the IFIs have not taken all possible steps to avoid the breaches concerned.

- *Guiding Principle 11*: **Attribution of Conduct and Corresponding Responsibility to Member States**
  IFI Member States shall be held responsible when conduct – be it action or omission – a) is performed in an area where they are factually in control, b) leads to the non-prevention or actual occurrence of breaches of international human rights law, and c) is attributable to them under the under the law on the responsibility of States, while providing that d) a causal link between the act/omission and the actual violation can be reasonably established by independent third bodies and that e) the Member States have not taken all possible steps to avoid the breaches concerned.

- *Guiding Principle 12*: **Attribution of Conduct and Corresponding Shared Responsibility**
  The IFIs and their Member States shall accept shared responsibility, apportioned to the relative weight of their levels of factual control, when conduct – be it action or omission – a) is performed in an area where they are factually in control, b) leads to the non-prevention or actual occurrence of breaches of international human rights law, and c) is attributable to them under the under the law on the responsibility of States and the law of the responsibility of international organizations, while provided that d) a causal link between the act/omission and the actual violation can be reasonably established by independent third bodies and that e) both the IFIs and the Member States have not taken all possible steps to avoid the breaches concerned.

- *Guiding Principle 13*: **Responsibility for Conduct of Private Subcontractors**
  Where human rights are violated by private subcontractors standing in a *direct* relationship to either the WBG or the IMF, the latter shall accept responsibility for having selected and funded the subcontractor and shall respond, together with the private actor concerned, to the human rights violations stemming from their conduct. In case of an *indirect* relationship, responsibility for the human rights violation shall be allocated proportional to the level of authority and factual control that the WBG or the IMF has over the subcontractor. The same applies, *mutatis mutandis*, to their Member States, when contracting private subcontractors for the execution of the relevant IFI's policies, projects and programs.

- *Guiding Principle 14*: **Debarring Private Sub-Contractors**
  In line with the 2010 agreement on cross-debarring firms (and individuals) found to have engaged in fraud and corruption in development projects funded by the IFIs, the latter should develop equal 'black lists' for firms found to have committed significant human rights violations.

3. ACCOUNTABILITY AND REMEDIES

- *Guiding Principle 15*: **Human Rights Impact Assessment**
  The WBG and the IMF and their Member States have a duty of due diligence in the monitoring and assessment of the human rights impact of their policies, projects and programs, and should conduct a tailor-made country- as well as situation-specific human rights impact assessment for each project and programme in advance of decisions on its undertaking. Such human rights impact assessments should also be made prior to any major policy decision.

- *Guiding Principle 16*: **Availability of Accountability Mechanisms**
  In advance of each project, the WBG and the IMF shall collaborate with stakeholders to establish non-judicial accountability mechanisms, such as grievance and complaints mechanisms, fact-finding missions, and mediation procedures, which are capable of adequately addressing human rights violations potentially caused in the course of the project and programme. The duty-holders and their stakeholders shall jointly determine which accountability mechanisms are most appropriate in particular cases.

- *Guiding Principle 17*: **Accessibility of Accountability Mechanisms**
  The WBG and the IMF shall ensure that all accountability mechanisms are easily accessible and affordable for affected individuals and groups, *inter alia*, through supporting capacity building initiatives that enable them to engage more effectively with both IFIs. Particular attention must be paid to those individuals and groups that are most vulnerable to potential human rights violations in the societies to which they belong.

- *Guiding Principle 18*: **Engagement with Civil Society**
  The WBG and the IMF should further support initiatives in which co-operation with civil society is strengthened in order to maximise their effective engagement with both IFIs and the communities affected by activities funded by the WBG and IMF.

- *Guiding Principle 19*: **Broadening the Mandate of the WBG Inspection Panel**
  Following its own position-taking on human rights issues, the WBG should include explicitly in the Inspection Panel's mandate the competence to address human rights violations linked to WBG projects and programs and projects, including the option of complaints about human rights related issues to be lodged by affected parties.

- *Guiding Principle 20*: **WBG and Private Sector Accountability**
  Where claims of individuals relate to the private sector lending activities of the WBG, the IFC/MIGA CAO shall address any adverse human rights impacts arising from their policies, project and programs and assist claimants with their search for reparation.

- *Guiding Principle 21*: **IMF Accountability Mechanisms**
  The IMF must review its accountability mechanisms in order to provide for the settlement of human rights complaints brought by individuals and communities that have been adversely impacted by the IMF's policies, projects or programs. Such a review could operate under an expectation that the IMF should, as a minimum, align its procedures of accountability with developments in the WBG.

- *Guiding Principle 22*: **Providing Reparation**
  Where expected negative human rights impacts do not lead to the cancellation of the project or program, or where human rights violations do actually occur, both IFIs and their Member States shall provide reparation, apportioned to their level of factual control. Where full reparation cannot be undertaken, compensation or other forms of reparation shall be provided.

ANNEX II

DRAFT ARTICLES ON THE RESPONSIBILITY OF STATES FOR INTERNATIONALLY WRONGFUL ACTS (2001) (EXCERPTS)

Text adopted by the International Law Commission of the United Nations at its fifty-third session, in 2001, and submitted to the General Assembly as a part of the Commission's report covering the work of that session. The report also contains commentaries on the draft articles. The text can be found at http://legal.un.org/ilc/texts/instruments/english/draft%20articles/9_6_2001.pdf. The General Assembly 'took note' of the Draft Articles and 'commen[ded] them to the attention of Governments without prejudice to the question of their future adoption or other appropriate action' (GA Res. 56/83, 12 December 2001). A few exceptions left aside not relevant in the present context, the Draft Articles are generally considered to be customary international law.

Article 1

Responsibility of a State for its internationally wrongful acts

Every internationally wrongful act of a State entails the international responsibility of that State.

Article 2

Elements of an internationally wrongful act of a State

There is an internationally wrongful act of a State when conduct consisting of an action or omission:

(a) is attributable to the State under international law; and
(b) constitutes a breach of an international obligation of the State.

Article 3

Characterization of an act of a State as internationally wrongful

The characterization of an act of a State as internationally wrongful is governed by international law. Such characterization is not affected by the characterization of the same act as lawful by internal law.

Article 4

Conduct of organs of a State

1. The conduct of any State organ shall be considered an act of that State under international law, whether the organ exercises legislative, executive, judicial or any other functions, whatever position it holds in the organization of the State, and whatever its character as an organ of the central Government or of a territorial unit of the State.
2. An organ includes any person or entity which has that status in accordance with the internal law of the State.

Article 5

Conduct of persons or entities exercising elements of governmental authority

The conduct of a person or entity which is not an organ of the State under article 4 but which is empowered by the law of that State to exercise elements of the governmental authority shall be considered an act of the State under international law, provided the person or entity is acting in that capacity in the particular instance.

Article 7

Excess of authority or contravention of instructions

The conduct of an organ of a State or of a person or entity empowered to exercise elements of the governmental authority shall be considered an act of the State under international law if the organ, person or entity acts in that capacity, even if it exceeds its authority or contravenes instructions.

Article 8

Conduct directed or controlled by a State

The conduct of a person or group of persons shall be considered an act of a State under international law if the person or group of persons is in fact acting on the instructions of, or under the direction or control of, that State in carrying out the conduct.

Article 12

Existence of a breach of an international obligation

There is a breach of an international obligation by a State when an act of that State is not in conformity with what is required of it by that obligation, regardless of its origin or character.

Article 14

Extension in time of the breach of an international obligation

1. The breach of an international obligation by an act of a State not having a continuing character occurs at the moment when the act is performed, even if its effects continue.

2. The breach of an international obligation by an act of a State having a continuing character extends over the entire period during which the act continues and remains not in conformity with the international obligation.
3. The breach of an international obligation requiring a State to prevent a given event occurs when the event occurs and extends over the entire period during which the event continues and remains not in conformity with that obligation.

Article 16
Aid or assistance in the commission of an internationally wrongful act
A State which aids or assists another State in the commission of an internationally wrongful act by the latter is internationally responsible for doing so if:
(a) that State does so with knowledge of the circumstances of the internationally wrongful act; and
(b) the act would be internationally wrongful if committed by that State.

Article 17
Direction and control exercised over the commission of an internationally wrongful act
A State which directs and controls another State in the commission of an internationally wrongful act by the latter is internationally responsible for that act if:
(a) that State does so with knowledge of the circumstances of the internationally wrongful act; and
(b) the act would be internationally wrongful if committed by that State.

Article 26
Compliance with peremptory norms
Nothing in this chapter [on circumstances precluding wrongfulness] precludes the wrongfulness of any act of a State which is not in conformity with an obligation arising under a peremptory norm of general international law.

Article 29
Continued duty of performance
The legal consequences of an internationally wrongful act under this part [on content of the international responsibility of a state] do not affect the continued duty of the responsible State to perform the obligation breached.

Article 30
Cessation and non-repetition
The State responsible for the internationally wrongful act is under an obligation:

(a) to cease that act, if it is continuing;
(b) to offer appropriate assurances and guarantees of non-repetition, if circumstances so require.

Article 31
Reparation
1. The responsible State is under an obligation to make full reparation for the injury caused by the internationally wrongful act.
2. Injury includes any damage, whether material or moral, caused by the internationally wrongful act of a State.

Article 32
Irrelevance of internal law
The responsible State may not rely on the provisions of its internal law as justification for failure to comply with its obligations under this part.

Article 33
Scope of international obligations set out in this part [on content of the international responsibility of a state]
1. The obligations of the responsible State set out in this part may be owed to another State, to several States, or to the international community as a whole, depending in particular on the character and content of the international obligation and on the circumstances of the breach.
2. This part is without prejudice to any right, arising from the international responsibility of a State, which may accrue directly to any person or entity other than a State.

Article 34
Forms of reparation
Full reparation for the injury caused by the internationally wrongful act shall take the form of restitution, compensation and satisfaction, either singly or in combination, in accordance with the provisions of this chapter.

Article 35
Restitution
A State responsible for an internationally wrongful act is under an obligation to make restitution, that is, to re-establish the situation which existed before the wrongful act was committed, provided and to the extent that restitution:
(a) is not materially impossible;
(b) does not involve a burden out of all proportion to the benefit deriving from restitution instead of compensation.

Article 36

Compensation

1. The State responsible for an internationally wrongful act is under an obligation to compensate for the damage caused thereby, insofar as such damage is not made good by restitution.
2. The compensation shall cover any financially assessable damage including loss of profits insofar as it is established.

Article 37

Satisfaction

1. The State responsible for an internationally wrongful act is under an obligation to give satisfaction for the injury caused by that act insofar as it cannot be made good by restitution or compensation.
2. Satisfaction may consist in an acknowledgement of the breach, an expression of regret, a formal apology or another appropriate modality.
3. Satisfaction shall not be out of proportion to the injury and may not take a form humiliating to the responsible State.

Article 38

Interest

1. Interest on any principal sum due under this chapter [on reparations for injury] shall be payable when necessary in order to ensure full reparation. The interest rate and mode of calculation shall be set so as to achieve that result.
2. Interest runs from the date when the principal sum should have been paid until the date the obligation to pay is fulfilled.

Article 39

Contribution to the injury

In the determination of reparation, account shall be taken of the contribution to the injury by wilful or negligent action or omission of the injured State or any person or entity in relation to whom reparation is sought.

Article 40

Application of this chapter [on serious breaches of obligations under peremptory norms of general international law]

1. This chapter applies to the international responsibility which is entailed by a serious breach by a State of an obligation arising under a peremptory norm of general international law.
2. A breach of such an obligation is serious if it involves a gross or systematic failure by the responsible State to fulfil the obligation.

Article 41

Particular consequences of a serious breach of an obligation under this chapter

1. States shall cooperate to bring to an end through lawful means any serious breach within the meaning of article 40.
2. No State shall recognize as lawful a situation created by a serious breach within the meaning of article 40, nor render aid or assistance in maintaining that situation.
3. This article is without prejudice to the other consequences referred to in this part [on content of the international responsibility of a state] and to such further consequences that a breach to which this chapter applies may entail under international law.

Article 42

Invocation of responsibility by an injured State

A State is entitled as an injured State to invoke the responsibility of another State if the obligation breached is owed to:

(a) that State individually; or

(b) a group of States including that State, or the international community as a whole, and the breach of the obligation:
   (i) specially affects that State; or
   (ii) is of such a character as radically to change the position of all the other States to which the obligation is owed with respect to the further performance of the obligation.

Article 46

Plurality of injured States

Where several States are injured by the same internationally wrongful act, each injured State may separately invoke the responsibility of the State which has committed the internationally wrongful act.

Article 47

Plurality of responsible States

1. Where several States are responsible for the same internationally wrongful act, the responsibility of each State may be invoked in relation to that act.
2. Paragraph 1:
   (a) does not permit any injured State to recover, by way of compensation, more than the damage it has suffered;
   (b) is without prejudice to any right of recourse against the other responsible States.

Article 48

Invocation of responsibility by a State other than an injured State

1. Any State other than an injured State is entitled to invoke the responsibility of another State in accordance with paragraph 2 if:
   (a) the obligation breached is owed to a group of States including that State, and is established for the protection of a collective interest of the group; or
   (b) the obligation breached is owed to the international community as a whole.
2. Any State entitled to invoke responsibility under paragraph 1 may claim from the responsible State:
   (a) cessation of the internationally wrongful act, and assurances and guarantees of non-repetition in accordance with article 30; and
   (b) performance of the obligation of reparation in accordance with the preceding articles, in the interest of the injured State or of the beneficiaries of the obligation breached.
3. [...]

Article 51

Proportionality

Countermeasures must be commensurate with the injury suffered, taking into account the gravity of the internationally wrongful act and the rights in question.

Article 55

Lex specialis

These articles do not apply where and to the extent that the conditions for the existence of an internationally wrongful act or the content or implementation of the international responsibility of a State are governed by special rules of international law.

Article 57

Responsibility of an international organization

These articles are without prejudice to any question of the responsibility under international law of an international organization, or of any State for the conduct of an international organization.

Article 58

Individual responsibility

These articles are without prejudice to any question of the individual responsibility under international law of any person acting on behalf of a State.

Article 59

Charter of the United Nations

These articles are without prejudice to the Charter of the United Nations

ANNEX III

DRAFT ARTICLES ON THE RESPONSIBILITY OF INTERNATIONAL ORGANIZATIONS (2011) (EXCERPTS)

Text adopted by the International Law Commission of the United Nations at its sixty-third session, in 2011, and submitted to the General Assembly as a part of the Commission's report covering the work of that session. The text can be found at http://legal.un.org/ilc/texts/instruments/english/draft%20articles/9_11_2011.pdf. A commentary can be found at http://legal.un.org/ilc/texts/instruments/english/draft%20articles/9_11_2011.pdf. The General Assembly 'took note' of the articles and 'commen[ded] them to the attention of Governments and international organizations without prejudice to the question of their future adoption or other appropriate action' (A/RES/66/100, 9 December 2011). Again, a few exceptions left aside not relevant in the present context, the Articles are generally considered to be customary international law.

Article 1

Scope of the present draft articles

1. The present draft articles apply to the international responsibility of an international organization for an internationally wrongful act.
2. The present draft articles also apply to the international responsibility of a State for an internationally wrongful act in connection with the conduct of an international organization.

Article 2

Use of terms for the purposes of the present draft articles

(a) 'international organization' means an organization established by a treaty or other instrument governed by international law and possessing its own international legal personality. International organizations may include as members, in addition to States, other entities;
(b) 'rules of the organization' means, in particular, the constituent instruments, decisions, resolutions and other acts of the international organization adopted in accordance with those instruments, and established practice of the organization;
(c) 'organ of an international organization' means any person or entity which has that status in accordance with the rules of the organization;
(d) 'agent of an international organization' means an official or other person or entity, other than an organ, who is charged by the organization with carrying

out, or helping to carry out, one of its functions, and thus through whom the organization acts.

Article 4

Elements of an internationally wrongful act of an international organization

There is an internationally wrongful act of an international organization when conduct consisting of an action or omission:

(a) is attributable to that organization under international law; and
(b) constitutes a breach of an international obligation of that organization.

Article 5

Characterization of an act of an international organization as internationally wrongful

The characterization of an act of an international organization as internationally wrongful is governed by international law.

Article 6

Conduct of organs or agents of an international organization

1. The conduct of an organ or agent of an international organization in the performance of functions of that organ or agent shall be considered an act of that organization under international law, whatever position the organ or agent holds in respect of the organization.
2. The rules of the organization apply in the determination of the functions of its organs and agents.

Article 8

Excess of authority or contravention of instructions

The conduct of an organ or agent of an international organization shall be considered an act of that organization under international law if the organ or agent acts in an official capacity and within the overall functions of that organization, even if the conduct exceeds the authority of that organ or agent or contravenes instructions.

Article 9

Conduct acknowledged and adopted by an international organization as its own

Conduct which is not attributable to an international organization under articles 6 to 8 shall nevertheless be considered an act of that organization under international law if and to the extent that the organization acknowledges and adopts the conduct in question as its own.

Article 10

Existence of a breach of an international obligation

1. There is a breach of an international obligation by an international organization when an act of that international organization is not in conformity with what is required of it by that obligation, regardless of the origin or character of the obligation concerned.
2. Paragraph 1 includes the breach of any international obligation that may arise for an international organization towards its members under the rules of the organization.

Article 11

International obligation in force for an international organization

An act of an international organization does not constitute a breach of an international obligation unless the organization is bound by the obligation in question at the time the act occurs.

Article 12

Extension in time of the breach of an international obligation

1. The breach of an international obligation by an act of an international organization not having a continuing character occurs at the moment when the act is performed, even if its effects continue.
2. The breach of an international obligation by an act of an international organization having a continuing character extends over the entire period during which the act continues and remains not in conformity with that obligation.
3. The breach of an international obligation requiring an international organization to prevent a given event occurs when the event occurs and extends over the entire period during which the event continues and remains not in conformity with that obligation.

Article 13

Breach consisting of a composite act

1. The breach of an international obligation by an international organization through a series of actions and omissions defined in aggregate as wrongful occurs when the action or omission occurs which, taken with the other actions or omissions, is sufficient to constitute the wrongful act.
2. In such a case, the breach extends over the entire period starting with the first of the actions or omissions of the series and lasts for as long as these actions or omissions are repeated and remain not in conformity with the international obligation.

Article 14

Aid or assistance in the commission of an internationally wrongful act

An international organization which aids or assists a State or another international organization in the commission of an internationally wrongful act by the State or the latter organization is internationally responsible for doing so if:

(a) the former organization does so with knowledge of the circumstances of the internationally wrongful act; and
(b) the act would be internationally wrongful if committed by that organization.

Article 15

Direction and control exercised over the commission of an internationally wrongful act

An international organization which directs and controls a State or another international organization in the commission of an internationally wrongful act by the State or the latter organization is internationally responsible for that act if:

(a) the former organization does so with knowledge of the circumstances of the internationally wrongful act; and
(b) the act would be internationally wrongful if committed by that organization.

Article 17

Circumvention of international obligations through decisions and authorizations addressed to members

1. An international organization incurs international responsibility if it circumvents one of its international obligations by adopting a decision binding member States or international organizations to commit an act that would be internationally wrongful if committed by the former organization.
2. An international organization incurs international responsibility if it circumvents one of its international obligations by authorizing member States or international organizations to commit an act that would be internationally wrongful if committed by the former organization and the act in question is committed because of that authorization.
3. Paragraphs 1 and 2 apply whether or not the act in question is internationally wrongful for the member States or international organizations to which the decision or authorization is addressed.

Article 26

Compliance with peremptory norms

Nothing in this Chapter [on circumstances precluding wrongfulness] precludes the wrongfulness of any act of an international organization which is not in conformity with an obligation arising under a peremptory norm of general international law.

Article 29

Continued duty of performance

The legal consequences of an internationally wrongful act under this Part [on content of the international responsibility of an international organization] do not affect the continued duty of the responsible international organization to perform the obligation breached.

Article 30

Cessation and non-repetition

The international organization responsible for the internationally wrongful act is under an obligation:

(a) to cease that act, if it is continuing;
(b) to offer appropriate assurances and guarantees of non-repetition, if circumstances so require.

Article 31

Reparation

1. The responsible international organization is under an obligation to make full reparation for the injury caused by the internationally wrongful act.
2. Injury includes any damage, whether material or moral, caused by the internationally wrongful act of an international organization.

Article 32

Relevance of the rules of the organization

1. The responsible international organization may not rely on its rules as justification for failure to comply with its obligations under this Part [on content of the international responsibility of an international organization].
2. Paragraph 1 is without prejudice to the applicability of the rules of an international organization to the relations between the organization and its member States and organizations.

Article 33

Scope of international obligations set out in this Part [on content of the international responsibility of an international organization]

1. The obligations of the responsible international organization set out in this Part may be owed to one or more States, to one or more other organizations, or to the international community as a whole, depending in particular on the character and content of the international obligation and on the circumstances of the breach.
2. This Part is without prejudice to any right, arising from the international responsibility of an international organization, which may accrue directly to any person or entity other than a State or an international organization.

Article 34

Forms of reparation

Full reparation for the injury caused by the internationally wrongful act shall take the form of restitution, compensation and satisfaction, either singly or in combination, in accordance with the provisions of this Chapter [on General Principles in relation to the international responsibility of an international organization].

Article 35

Restitution

An international organization responsible for an internationally wrongful act is under an obligation to make restitution, that is, to re-establish the situation which existed before the wrongful act was committed, provided and to the extent that restitution:

(a) is not materially impossible;

(b) does not involve a burden out of all proportion to the benefit deriving from restitution instead of compensation.

Article 36

Compensation

1. The international organization responsible for an internationally wrongful act is under an obligation to compensate for the damage caused thereby, insofar as such damage is not made good by restitution.
2. The compensation shall cover any financially assessable damage including loss of profits insofar as it is established.

Article 37

Satisfaction

1. The international organization responsible for an internationally wrongful act is under an obligation to give satisfaction for the injury caused by that act insofar as it cannot be made good by restitution or compensation.
2. Satisfaction may consist in an acknowledgement of the breach, an expression of regret, a formal apology or another appropriate modality.
3. Satisfaction shall not be out of proportion to the injury and may not take a form humiliating to the responsible international organization.

Article 39

Contribution to the injury

In the determination of reparation, account shall be taken of the contribution to the injury by wilful or negligent action or omission of the injured State or international organization or of any person or entity in relation to whom reparation is sought.

Article 40

Ensuring the fulfilment of the obligation to make reparation

1. The responsible international organization shall take all appropriate measures in accordance with its rules to ensure that its members provide it with the means for effectively fulfilling its obligations under this Chapter [on serious breaches of obligations under peremptory norms of general international law].
2. The members of a responsible international organization shall take all the appropriate measures that may be required by the rules of the organization in order to enable the organization to fulfil its obligations under this Chapter.

Article 41

Application of this Chapter [on serious breaches of obligations under peremptory norms of general international law]

1. This Chapter applies to the international responsibility which is entailed by a serious breach by an international organization of an obligation arising under a peremptory norm of general international law.
2. A breach of such an obligation is serious if it involves a gross or systematic failure by the responsible international organization to fulfil the obligation.

Article 43

Invocation of responsibility by an injured State or international organization

A State or an international organization is entitled as an injured State or an injured international organization to invoke the responsibility of another international organization if the obligation breached is owed to:

(a) that State or the former international organization individually;

(b) a group of States or international organizations including that State or the former international organization, or the international community as a whole, and the breach of the obligation:

   (i) specially affects that State or that international organization; or

   (ii) is of such a character as radically to change the position of all the other States and international organizations to which the obligation is owed with respect to the further performance of the obligation.

Article 47

Plurality of injured States or international organizations

Where several States or international organizations are injured by the same internationally wrongful act of an international organization, each injured State or international organization may separately invoke the responsibility of the international organization for the internationally wrongful act.

Article 48

Responsibility of an international organization and one or more States or international organizations

1. Where an international organization and one or more States or other international organizations are responsible for the same internationally wrongful act, the responsibility of each State or organization may be invoked in relation to that act.
2. Subsidiary responsibility may be invoked insofar as the invocation of the primary responsibility has not led to reparation.
3. Paragraphs 1 and 2:
   (a) do not permit any injured State or international organization to recover, by way of compensation, more than the damage it has suffered;
   (b) are without prejudice to any right of recourse that the State or international organization providing reparation may have against the other responsible States or international organizations.

Article 49

Invocation of responsibility by a State or an international organization other than an injured State or international organization

1. A State or an international organization other than an injured State or international organization is entitled to invoke the responsibility of another international organization in accordance with paragraph 4 if the obligation breached is owed to a group of States or international organizations, including the State or organization that invokes responsibility, and is established for the protection of a collective interest of the group.
2. A State other than an injured State is entitled to invoke the responsibility of an international organization in accordance with paragraph 4 if the obligation breached is owed to the international community as a whole.
3. An international organization other than an injured international organization is entitled to invoke the responsibility of another international organization in accordance with paragraph 4 if the obligation breached is owed to the international community as a whole and safeguarding the interest of the international community as a whole underlying the obligation breached is within the functions of the international organization invoking responsibility.
4. A State or an international organization entitled to invoke responsibility under paragraphs 1 to 3 may claim from the responsible international organization:
   (a) cessation of the internationally wrongful act, and assurances and guarantees of non-repetition in accordance with draft article 30; and
   (b) performance of the obligation of reparation in accordance with Part Three [on content of the international responsibility of an international organization], in the interest of the injured State or international organization or of the beneficiaries of the obligation breached.
5. […]

Article 58

Aid or assistance by a State in the commission of an internationally wrongful act by an international organization

1. A State which aids or assists an international organization in the commission of an internationally wrongful act by the latter is internationally responsible for doing so if:
   (a) the State does so with knowledge of the circumstances of the internationally wrongful act; and
   (b) the act would be internationally wrongful if committed by that State.
2. An act by a State member of an international organization done in accordance with the rules of the organization does not as such engage the international responsibility of that State under the terms of this article.

Article 59

Direction and control exercised by a State over the commission of an internationally wrongful act by an international organization

1. A State which directs and controls an international organization in the commission of an internationally wrongful act by the latter is internationally responsible for that act if:
   (a) the State does so with knowledge of the circumstances of the internationally wrongful act; and
   (b) the act would be internationally wrongful if committed by that State.
2. An act by a State member of an international organization done in accordance with the rules of the organization does not as such engage the international responsibility of that State under the terms of this draft article.

Article 60

Coercion of an international organization by a State

A State which coerces an international organization to commit an act is internationally responsible for that act if:

(a) the act would, but for the coercion, be an internationally wrongful act of the coerced international organization; and
(b) the coercing State does so with knowledge of the circumstances of the act.

Article 61

Circumvention of international obligations of a State member of an international organization

1. A State member of an international organization incurs international responsibility if, by taking advantage of the fact that the organization has competence in relation to the subject-matter of one of the State's international obligations, it circumvents that obligation by causing the organization to commit an act that, if committed by the State, would have constituted a breach of the obligation.

2. Paragraph 1 applies whether or not the act in question is internationally wrongful for the international organization.

Article 62

Responsibility of a State member of an international organization for an internationally wrongful act of that organization

1. A State member of an international organization is responsible for an internationally wrongful act of that organization if:
   (a) it has accepted responsibility for that act towards the injured party; or
   (b) it has led the injured party to rely on its responsibility.
2. Any international responsibility of a State under paragraph 1 is presumed to be subsidiary.

Article 64

Lex specialis

These draft articles do not apply where and to the extent that the conditions for the existence of an internationally wrongful act or the content or implementation of the international responsibility of an international organization, or of a State in connection with the conduct of an international organization, are governed by special rules of international law. Such special rules of international law may be contained in the rules of the organization applicable to the relations between an international organization and its members.

Article 65

Questions of international responsibility not regulated by these draft articles

The applicable rules of international law continue to govern questions concerning the responsibility of an international organization or a State for an internationally wrongful act to the extent that they are not regulated by these draft articles.

Article 66

Individual responsibility

These draft articles are without prejudice to any question of the individual responsibility under international law of any person acting on behalf of an international organization or a State.

Article 67

Charter of the United Nations

These draft articles are without prejudice to the Charter of the United Nations.

ANNEX IV

MAASTRICHT PRINCIPLES ON EXTRATERRITORIAL OBLIGATIONS OF STATES IN THE AREA OF ECONOMIC, SOCIAL AND CULTURAL RIGHTS (2011) (EXCERPTS)

The Maastricht Principles on Extraterritorial Obligations of States in the area of Economic, Social and Cultural Rights were adopted by a group of experts in international law and human rights at a gathering on 28 September 2011 organised by Maastricht University and the International Commission of Jurists. The experts came from universities and organisations located in all regions of the world and included current and former members of international human rights treaty bodies, regional human rights bodies, and former and current Special Rapporteurs of the United Nations Human Rights Council. Their work was based on legal research conducted over a period of more than a decade. The final version of the Principles, dated 29 February 2012, can be found at www.maastrichtuniversity.nl/web/Institutes/MaastrichtCentreForHumanRights/MaastrichtETOPrinciples.htm. Although not legally binding, the Principles are often (and increasingly) referred to in national and international legal and semi-legal practice. See www.etoconsortium.org/.

Principle 8

Definition of extraterritorial obligations

For the purposes of these Principles, extraterritorial obligations encompass:

a) obligations relating to the acts and omissions of a State, within or beyond its territory, that have effects on the enjoyment of human rights outside of that State's territory; and
b) obligations of a global character that are set out in the Charter of the United Nations and human rights instruments to take action, separately, and jointly through international cooperation, to realize human rights universally.

Principle 9

Scope of jurisdiction

A State has obligations to respect, protect and fulfil economic, social and cultural rights in any of the following:

a) situations over which it exercises authority or effective control, whether or not such control is exercised in accordance with international law;

b) situations over which State acts or omissions bring about foreseeable effects on the enjoyment of economic, social and cultural rights, whether within or outside its territory;
c) situations in which the State, acting separately or jointly, whether through its executive, legislative or judicial branches, is in a position to exercise decisive influence or to take measures to realize economic, social and cultural rights extraterritorially, in accordance with international law.

Principle 10

Limits to the entitlement to exercise jurisdiction

The State's obligation to respect, protect and fulfil economic, social and cultural rights extraterritorially does not authorize a State to act in violation of the UN Charter and general international law.

Principle 11

State responsibility

State responsibility is engaged as a result of conduct attributable to a State, acting separately or jointly with other States or entities, that constitutes a breach of its international human rights obligations whether within its territory or extraterritorially.

Principle 12

Attribution of State responsibility for the conduct of non-State actors

State responsibility extends to:

a) acts and omissions of non-State actors acting on the instructions or under the direction or control of the State; and
b) acts and omissions of persons or entities which are not organs of the State, such as corporations and other business enterprises, where they are empowered by the State to exercise elements of governmental authority, provided those persons or entities are acting in that capacity in the particular instance.

Principle 13

Obligation to avoid causing harm

States must desist from acts and omissions that create a real risk of nullifying or impairing the enjoyment of economic, social and cultural rights extraterritorially. The responsibility of States is engaged where such nullification or impairment is a foreseeable result of their conduct. Uncertainty about potential impacts does not constitute justification for such conduct.

Principle 14
Impact assessment and prevention
States must conduct prior assessment, with public participation, of the risks and potential extraterritorial impacts of their laws, policies and practices on the enjoyment of economic, social and cultural rights. The results of the assessment must be made public. The assessment must also be undertaken to inform the measures that States must adopt to prevent violations or ensure their cessation as well as to ensure effective remedies.

Principle 15
Obligations of States as members of international organizations
As a member of an international organization, the State remains responsible for its own conduct in relation to its human rights obligations within its territory and extraterritorially. A State that transfers competences to, or participates in, an international organization must take all reasonable steps to ensure that the relevant organization acts consistently with the international human rights obligations of that State.

Principle 16
Obligations of international organizations
The present Principles apply to States without excluding their applicability to the human rights obligations of international organizations under, inter alia, general international law and international agreements to which they are parties.

Principle 17
International agreements
States must elaborate, interpret and apply relevant international agreements and standards in a manner consistent with their human rights obligations. Such obligations include those pertaining to international trade, investment, finance, taxation, environmental protection, development cooperation, and security.

Principle 19
General obligation [in relation to the obligations to respect human rights]
All States must take action, separately, and jointly through international cooperation, to respect the economic, social and cultural rights of persons within their territories and extraterritorially [...].

Principle 20
Direct interference
All States have the obligation to refrain from conduct which nullifies or impairs the enjoyment and exercise of economic, social and cultural rights of persons outside their territories.

Principle 21

Indirect interference

States must refrain from any conduct which:

a) impairs the ability of another State or international organization to comply with that State's or that international organization's obligations as regards economic, social and cultural rights; or
b) aids, assists, directs, controls or coerces another State or international organization to breach that State's or that international organization's obligations as regards economic, social and cultural rights, where the former States do so with knowledge of the circumstances of the act.

Principle 23

General obligation [in relation to the obligations to protect human rights]

All States must take action, separately, and jointly through international cooperation, to protect economic, social and cultural rights of persons within their territories and extraterritorially, as set out in Principles 24 to 27.

Principle 24

Obligation to regulate

All States must take necessary measures to ensure that non-State actors which they are in a position to regulate, as set out in Principle 25, such as private individuals and organizations, and transnational corporations and other business enterprises, do not nullify or impair the enjoyment of economic, social and cultural rights. These include administrative, legislative, investigative, adjudicatory and other measures. All other States have a duty to refrain from nullifying or impairing the discharge of this obligation to protect.

Principle 25

Bases for protection

States must adopt and enforce measures to protect economic, social and cultural rights through legal and other means, including diplomatic means, in each of the following circumstances:

a) the harm or threat of harm originates or occurs on its territory;
b) where the non-State actor has the nationality of the State concerned;
c) as regards business enterprises, where the corporation, or its parent or controlling company, has its centre of activity, is registered or domiciled, or has its main place of business or substantial business activities, in the State concerned;
d) where there is a reasonable link between the State concerned and the conduct it seeks to regulate, including where relevant aspects of a non-State actor's activities are carried out in that State's territory;

e) where any conduct impairing economic, social and cultural rights constitutes a violation of a peremptory norm of international law. Where such a violation also constitutes a crime under international law, States must exercise universal jurisdiction over those bearing responsibility or lawfully transfer them to an appropriate jurisdiction.

Principle 26
Position to influence
States that are in a position to influence the conduct of non-State actors even if they are not in a position to regulate such conduct, such as through their public procurement system or international diplomacy, should exercise such influence, in accordance with the Charter of the United Nations and general international law, in order to protect economic, social and cultural rights.

Principle 27
Obligation to cooperate
All States must cooperate to ensure that non-State actors do not impair the enjoyment of the economic, social and cultural rights of any persons. This obligation includes measures to prevent human rights abuses by non-State actors, to hold them to account for any such abuses, and to ensure an effective remedy for those affected.

Principle 28
General obligation [in relation to obligations to fulfil human rights]
All States must take action, separately, and jointly through international cooperation, to fulfil economic, social and cultural rights of persons within their territories and extraterritorially, as set out in Principles 29 to 35.

Principle 29
Obligation to create an international enabling environment
States must take deliberate, concrete and targeted steps, separately, and jointly through international cooperation, to create an international enabling environment conducive to the universal fulfilment of economic, social and cultural rights, including in matters relating to bilateral and multilateral trade, investment, taxation, finance, environmental protection, and development cooperation.

The compliance with this obligation is to be achieved through, *inter alia*:

a) elaboration, interpretation, application and regular review of multilateral and bilateral agreements as well as international standards;
b) measures and policies by each State in respect of its foreign relations, including actions within international organizations, and its domestic measures and policies that can contribute to the fulfilment of economic, social and cultural rights extraterritorially.

Principle 30

Coordination and allocation of responsibilities

States should coordinate with each other, including in the allocation of responsibilities, in order to cooperate effectively in the universal fulfilment of economic, social and cultural rights. The lack of such coordination does not exonerate a State from giving effect to its separate extraterritorial obligations.

Principle 31

Capacity and resources

A State has the obligation to fulfil economic, social and cultural rights in its territory to the maximum of its ability. Each State must separately and, where necessary, jointly contribute to the fulfilment of economic, social and cultural rights extraterritorially, commensurate with, *inter alia*, its economic, technical and technological capacities, available resources, and influence in international decision-making processes. States must cooperate to mobilize the maximum of available resources for the universal fulfilment of economic, social and cultural rights.

Principle 32

Principles and priorities in cooperation

In fulfilling economic, social and cultural rights extraterritorially, States must:

a) prioritize the realization of the rights of disadvantaged, marginalized and vulnerable groups;
b) prioritize core obligations to realize minimum essential levels of economic, social and cultural rights, and move as expeditiously and effectively as possible towards the full realization of economic, social and cultural rights;
c) observe international human rights standards, including the right to self-determination and the right to participate in decision-making, as well as the principles of non-discrimination and equality, including gender equality, transparency, and accountability; and
d) avoid any retrogressive measures or else discharge their burden to demonstrate that such measures are duly justified by reference to the full range of human rights obligations, and are only taken after a comprehensive examination of alternatives.

Principle 33

Obligation to provide international assistance

As part of the broader obligation of international cooperation, States, acting separately and jointly, that are in a position to do so, must provide international assistance to contribute to the fulfilment of economic, social and cultural rights in other States, in a manner consistent with Principle 32.

Principle 34

Obligation to seek international assistance and cooperation

A State has the obligation to seek international assistance and cooperation on mutually agreed terms when that State is unable, despite its best efforts, to guarantee economic, social and cultural rights within its territory. That State has an obligation to ensure that assistance provided is used towards the realization of economic, social and cultural rights.

Principle 35

Response to a request for international assistance or cooperation

States that receive a request to assist or cooperate and are in a position to do so must consider the request in good faith, and respond in a manner consistent with their obligations to fulfil economic, social and cultural rights extraterritorially. In responding to the request, States must be guided by Principles 31 and 32.

Principle 36

Accountability

States must ensure the availability of effective mechanisms to provide for accountability in the discharge of their extraterritorial obligations. In order to ensure the effectiveness of such mechanisms, States must establish systems and procedures for the full and thorough monitoring of compliance with their human rights obligations, including through national human rights institutions acting in conformity with the United Nations Principles relating to the Status of National Institutions (Paris Principles).

Principle 37

General obligation to provide effective remedy

States must ensure the enjoyment of the right to a prompt, accessible and effective remedy before an independent authority, including, where necessary, recourse to a judicial authority, for violations of economic, social and cultural rights. Where the harm resulting from an alleged violation has occurred on the territory of a State other than a State in which the harmful conduct took place, any State concerned must provide remedies to the victim.

To give effect to this obligation, States should:

a) seek cooperation and assistance from other concerned States where necessary to ensure a remedy;
b) ensure remedies are available for groups as well as individuals;
c) ensure the participation of victims in the determination of appropriate remedies;
d) ensure access to remedies, both judicial and non-judicial, at the national and international levels; and
e) accept the right of individual complaints and develop judicial remedies at the international level.

Principle 38

Effective remedies and reparation

Remedies, to be effective, must be capable of leading to a prompt, thorough and impartial investigation; cessation of the violation if it is ongoing; and adequate reparation, including, as necessary, restitution, compensation, satisfaction, rehabilitation and guarantees of non-repetition. To avoid irreparable harm, interim measures must be available and States must respect the indication of interim measures by a competent judicial or quasi-judicial body. Victims have the right to truth about the facts and circumstances surrounding the violations, which should also be disclosed to the public, provided that it causes no further harm to the victim.

Principle 39

Inter-State complaints mechanisms

States should avail themselves of, and cooperate with, inter-State complaints mechanisms, including human rights mechanisms, to ensure reparation for any violation of an extraterritorial obligation relating to economic, social and cultural rights. States should seek reparation in the interest of injured persons as beneficiaries under the relevant treaties addressing economic, social and cultural rights, and should take into account, wherever feasible, the views of injured persons with regard to the reparation to be sought. Reparation for the injuries obtained from the responsible State should be transferred to the injured persons.

Principle 40

Non-judicial accountability mechanisms

In addition to the requisite judicial remedies, States should make non-judicial remedies available, which may include, inter alia, access to complaints mechanisms established under the auspices of international organizations, national human rights institutions or ombudspersons, and ensure that these remedies comply with the requirements of effective remedies under Principle 37. States should ensure additional accountability measures are in place at the domestic level, such as access to a parliamentary body tasked with monitoring governmental policies, as well as at the international level.

Principle 41

Reporting and monitoring

States must cooperate with international and regional human rights mechanisms, including periodic reporting and inquiry procedures of treaty bodies and mechanisms of the UN Human Rights Council, and peer review mechanisms, on the implementation of their extraterritorial obligations in relation to economic, social and cultural rights, and redress instances of noncompliance as identified by these mechanisms.

ANNEX V
UN GUIDING PRINCIPLES ON BUSINESS AND HUMAN RIGHTS (2011) (EXCERPTS)

The UN Guiding Principles on Business and Human Rights were developed as a (key) step in the implementation of the UN 'Protect, Respect and Remedy' framework for business and human rights, as developed in 2008 by the UN Special Representative for this issue, John Ruggie. The Principles have been endorsed by the UN Human Rights Council (HRC/RES/17/4, 16 June 2011), and the Council also established the UN Working Group on business and human rights, requesting it, *inter alia*, to promote the dissemination and implementation of the Principles; to identify good practices and lessons learned; to 'continue to explore options and make recommendations at the national, regional and international levels for enhancing access to effective remedies available to those whose human rights are affected by corporate activities, including those in conflict areas' (*ibidem*). The Principles, including Commentaries, can be found at www.ohchr.org/documents/publications/GuidingprinciplesBusinesshr_en.pdf.

The UN Guiding Principles follow the division in terms of (a) the State duty to protect human rights, (b) corporate responsibility to respect human rights, and (c) access to remedy, to be taken care of by both states and business enterprises. The Principles are divided into 'foundational' and 'operational' principles; however, this division is left aside here. Italics have been added in order to facilitate reading/browsing of this annex.

I. THE STATE DUTY TO PROTECT HUMAN RIGHTS

Principle 1
States must *protect* against human rights abuse within their territory and/or jurisdiction by third parties, including business enterprises. This requires taking appropriate steps to prevent, investigate, punish and redress such abuse through effective policies, legislation, regulations and adjudication.

Principle 2
States should *set out* clearly the *expectation* that all business enterprises domiciled in their territory and/or jurisdiction respect human rights throughout their operations.

Principle 4

States should take *additional steps* to protect against human rights abuses by *business enterprises that are owned or controlled by the State*, or that receive substantial support and services from State agencies such as export credit agencies and official investment insurance or guarantee agencies, including, where appropriate, by requiring *human rights due diligence.*

Principle 5

States should exercise *adequate oversight* in order to meet their international human rights obligations when they contract with, or legislate for, business enterprises to provide services that may impact upon the enjoyment of human rights.

Principle 6

States should *promote respect* for human rights by business enterprises with which they conduct *commercial transactions.*

Principle 7

Because the risk of gross human rights abuses is heightened in *conflict-affected areas*, States should help ensure that business enterprises operating in those contexts are not involved with such abuses, including by:

(a) Engaging at the earliest stage possible with business enterprises to help them identify, prevent and mitigate the human rights-related risks of their activities and business relationships;

(b) Providing adequate assistance to business enterprises to assess and address the heightened risks of abuses, paying special attention to both gender-based and sexual violence;

(c) Denying access to public support and services for a business enterprise that is involved with gross human rights abuses and refuses to cooperate in addressing the situation;

(d) Ensuring that their current policies, legislation, regulations and enforcement measures are effective in addressing the risk of business involvement in gross human rights abuses.

Principle 9

States should maintain *adequate domestic policy space* to meet their human rights obligations when pursuing business-related policy objectives with other States or business enterprises, for instance through *investment treaties or contracts.*

Principle 10

States, *when acting as members of multilateral institutions* that deal with business-related issues, should:

(a) Seek to ensure that those institutions neither restrain the ability of their member States to meet their duty to protect nor hinder business enterprises from respecting human rights;
(b) Encourage those institutions, within their respective mandates and capacities, to promote business respect for human rights and, where requested, to help States meet their duty to protect against human rights abuse by business enterprises, including through technical assistance, capacity-building and awareness-raising;
(c) Draw on these Guiding Principles to promote shared understanding and advance international cooperation in the management of business and human rights challenges.

II. THE CORPORATE RESPONSIBILITY TO RESPECT HUMAN RIGHTS

Principle 11

Business enterprises should *respect* human rights. This means that they should avoid infringing on the human rights of others and should address adverse human rights impacts with which they are involved.

Principle 12

The responsibility of business enterprises to respect human rights refers to *internationally recognized human rights* – understood, *at a minimum*, as those expressed in the International Bill of Human Rights and the principles concerning fundamental rights set out in the International Labour Organization's Declaration on Fundamental Principles and Rights at Work.

Principle 13

The responsibility to respect human rights requires that business enterprises:
(a) *Avoid causing or contributing to adverse human rights impacts* through their own activities, and address such impacts when they occur;
(b) Seek to *prevent or mitigate* adverse human rights impacts that are directly linked to their operations, products or services by their business relationships, even if they have not contributed to those impacts.

Principle 14

The responsibility of business enterprises to respect human rights applies to *all enterprises regardless of their size, sector, operational context, ownership and structure*. Nevertheless, the scale and complexity of the means through which enterprises meet that responsibility may vary according to these factors and with the severity of the enterprise's adverse human rights impacts.

Principle 15

In order to meet their responsibility to respect human rights, business enterprises *should have in place policies and processes* appropriate to their size and circumstances, including:

(a) A policy commitment to meet their responsibility to respect human rights;
(b) A human rights due diligence process to identify, prevent, mitigate and account for how they address their impacts on human rights;
(c) Processes to enable the remediation of any adverse human rights impacts they cause or to which they contribute.

Principle 16

As the basis for embedding their responsibility to respect human rights, business enterprises should express their commitment to meet this responsibility through a *statement of policy* that:

(a) Is approved at the *most senior level* of the business enterprise;
(b) Is *informed by* relevant internal and/or external *expertise*;
(c) Stipulates the enterprise's human rights *expectations of personnel, business partners* and other parties directly linked to its operations, products or services;
(d) Is *publicly available* and communicated internally and externally to all personnel, business partners and other relevant parties;
(e) Is reflected in *operational policies and procedures* necessary to embed it throughout the business enterprise.

Principle 17

In order to identify, prevent, mitigate and account for how they address their adverse human rights impacts, business enterprises should carry out *human rights due diligence*. The process should include assessing actual and potential human rights impacts, integrating and acting upon the findings, tracking responses, and communicating how impacts are addressed. Human rights due diligence:

(a) Should *cover adverse human rights impacts* that the business enterprise may cause or contribute to through its own activities, or which may be directly linked to its operations, products or services by its business relationships;
(b) Will *vary in complexity* with the size of the business enterprise, the risk of severe human rights impacts, and the nature and context of its operations;
(c) Should be *ongoing*, recognizing that the human rights risks may change over time as the business enterprise's operations and operating context evolve.

Principle 18

In order to gauge human rights risks, business enterprises should *identify and assess any actual or potential adverse human rights impacts* with which they may be involved either through their own activities or as a result of their business relationships. This process should:

(a) Draw on internal and/or *independent external human rights expertise*;
(b) Involve *meaningful consultation with potentially affected groups* and other relevant *stakeholders*, as appropriate to the size of the business enterprise and the nature and context of the operation.

Principle 19

In order to *prevent and mitigate* adverse human rights impacts, business enterprises should integrate the findings from their impact assessments across relevant internal functions and processes, and take appropriate action.

(a) Effective integration requires that:
 (i) Responsibility for addressing such impacts is assigned to the appropriate level and function within the business enterprise;
 (ii) Internal decision-making, budget allocations and oversight processes enable effective responses to such impacts.
(b) Appropriate action will vary according to:
 (i) Whether the business enterprise causes or contributes to an adverse impact, or whether it is involved solely because the impact is directly linked to its operations, products or services by a business relationship;
 (ii) The extent of its leverage in addressing the adverse impact.

Principle 20

In order to verify whether adverse human rights impacts are being addressed, business enterprises should *track the effectiveness of their response*. Tracking should:

(a) Be based on appropriate qualitative and quantitative indicators;
(b) Draw on feedback from both internal and external sources, including affected stakeholders.

Principle 21

In order to account for how they address their human rights impacts, business enterprises should be prepared to *communicate* this *externally*, particularly when concerns are raised by or on behalf of *affected stakeholders*. Business enterprises whose operations or operating contexts pose risks of severe human rights impacts should report formally on how they address them. In all instances, communications should:

(a) Be of a form and frequency that reflect an enterprise's human rights impacts and that are accessible to its intended audiences;
(b) Provide information that is sufficient to evaluate the adequacy of an enterprise's response to the particular human rights impact involved;
(c) In turn not pose risks to affected stakeholders, personnel or to legitimate requirements of commercial confidentiality.

Principle 22
Where business enterprises identify that they have caused or contributed to adverse impacts, they should *provide for or cooperate* in their *remediation* through legitimate processes.

Principle 23
In all contexts, business enterprises should:
(a) *Comply with* all applicable laws and respect *internationally recognized human rights*, wherever they operate;
(b) Seek ways to *honour the principles of internationally recognized human rights* when faced with *conflicting requirements*;
(c) Treat the risk of causing or contributing to gross human rights abuses as a *legal compliance issue* wherever they operate.

Principle 24
Where it is necessary to prioritize actions to address actual and potential adverse human rights impacts, business enterprises should *first seek to prevent and mitigate those that are most severe* or where delayed response would make them irremediable.

III. ACCESS TO REMEDY

Principle 25
As part of their duty to protect against business-related human rights abuse, *States* must take appropriate steps to ensure, through judicial, administrative, legislative or other appropriate means, that when such abuses occur within their territory and/or jurisdiction those affected have *access to effective remedy.*

Principle 26
States should take appropriate steps to ensure the *effectiveness of domestic judicial mechanisms* when addressing business-related human rights abuses, including considering ways to reduce legal, practical and other relevant barriers that could lead to a denial of access to remedy.

Principle 27
States should provide *effective and appropriate non-judicial grievance mechanisms,* alongside judicial mechanisms, as part of a comprehensive State-based system for the remedy of business-related human rights abuse.

Principle 28
States should consider ways to facilitate access to *effective non-State-based grievance mechanisms* dealing with business-related human rights harms.

Principle 29

To make it possible for grievances to be addressed early and remediated directly, *business enterprises* should establish or participate in *effective operational-level grievance mechanisms* for individuals and communities who may be adversely impacted.

Principle 31

In order to ensure their *effectiveness*, non-judicial grievance mechanisms, both State-based and non-State-based, should be:

(a) *Legitimate*: enabling trust from the stakeholder groups for whose use they are intended, and being accountable for the fair conduct of grievance processes;

(b) *Accessible*: being known to all stakeholder groups for whose use they are intended, and providing adequate assistance for those who may face particular barriers to access;

(c) *Predictable*: providing a clear and known procedure with an indicative time frame for each stage, and clarity on the types of process and outcome available and means of monitoring implementation;

(d) *Equitable*: seeking to ensure that aggrieved parties have reasonable access to sources of information, advice and expertise necessary to engage in a grievance process on fair, informed and respectful terms;

(e) *Transparent*: keeping parties to a grievance informed about its progress, and providing sufficient information about the mechanism's performance to build confidence in its effectiveness and meet any public interest at stake;

(f) *Rights-compatible*: ensuring that outcomes and remedies accord with internationally recognized human rights;

(g) *A source of continuous learning*: drawing on relevant measures to identify lessons for improving the mechanism and preventing future grievances and harms;

[...]

(h) Based on *engagement and dialogue*: consulting the *stakeholder groups* for whose use they are intended on their design and performance, and focusing on *dialogue* as the means to address and resolve grievances.

BIBLIOGRAPHY

This list of references covers all articles, reports and books that have been used in the course of this project. Resolutions, case law, speeches, factsheets, statutes and treaties referred to in the footnotes are not mentioned again.

Augenstein, Daniel, 'The Crisis of International Human Rights Law in the Global Market Economy', in: *Netherlands Yearbook of International Law 2013*, The Hague: Asser Press/Cambridge University Press/Springer, 2014.

Barros, Ana Sofia and Cedric Ryngaert, 'The Position of Member States in (Autonomous) Institutional Decision-Making: Implications for the Establishment of Responsibility', 11 *International Organizations Law Review*, 2014.

Berendsen, Bernard (ed.), *Economic Growth and the Common Good*, Amsterdam: KIT Publishers, 2010.

Berendsen, Bernard (ed.), *Common Goods in a Divided World*, Amsterdam: KIT Publishers, 2010.

Blake, Conway, *Normative Instruments in International Human Rights Law: Locating The General Comment*, Center For Human Rights And Global Justice Working Paper Number 17, New York, 2008.

Bradlow, Daniel, 'The World Bank, the IMF, and Human Rights', 6 *Journal of Transnational Law and Contemporary Problems*, 1996.

Bradlow, Daniel, 'The Reform of the Governance of the IFIs: A Critical Assessment', 3 *The World Bank Legal Review: International Financial Institutions and Global Legal Governance*, 2012.

Brown Weiss, Edith, Andres Rigo Sureda and Laurence Boisson de Chazournes (eds), *The World Bank, International Financial Institutions, and the Development of International Law*, Washington DC: The American Society of International Law, 1999, esp. Part 2.

Buchan, R., H. Jones and N.D. White, 'The Externalization of Peacekeeping: Policy, Responsibility and Accountability', 15 *Journal of International Peacekeeping*, 2011.

Centre on Housing Rights and Evictions, *Forced Evictions and Human Rights*, Geneva, 1999.

Cissé, H., 'Should the Political Prohibition in Charters of International Financial Institutions Be Revisited? The Case of the World Bank', 3 *The World Bank Legal Review: International Financial Institutions and Global Legal Governance*, 2012.

Clapham, A., *Human Rights Obligations of Non-State Actors*, Oxford: Oxford University Press, 2010.

Collier, Paul, *The Bottom Billion; Why the Poorest Countries Are Failing and What Can Be Done About it*, Oxford: Oxford University Press, 2008.

Coomans, Fons and Menno T. Kamminga (eds), *Extraterritorial Application of Human Rights Treaties*, Antwerp/Oxford: Intersentia, 2004.

Crawford, James, *The Rights of Peoples* (ed.), Oxford: Clarendon Press, 1988.

Crawford, James, *The International Law Commission's Articles on State Responsibility*, Cambridge: Cambridge University Press, 2002.

Crawford, James, *State Responsibility: The General Part*, Cambridge: Cambridge University Press, 2013.

Dao, Mai and Prakash Loungani, *The Human Cost of Recessions: Assessing it, Reducing it*, Washington: The International Monetary Fund, 2010.

Daniño, R., 'The Legal Aspects of the World Bank's Work on Human Rights: Some Preliminary Thoughts', in: Philip Alston and Mary Robinson (eds), *Human Rights and Development: Towards Mutual Reinforcement*, Oxford: Oxford University Press, 2005.

Darrow, Mac, *Between Light and Shadow; The World Bank, the International Monetary Fund and International Human Rights Law*, Oxford: Hart Publishing, 2003.

Darrow, Mac, 'World and International Monetary Fund', in: David Forsythe (Editor in Chief), *Encyclopedia of Human Rights* (2009 ff), Vol. 5, Oxford: Oxford University Press.

Dunoff, Jeffrey L. and Mark A. Pollack (eds), *Interdisciplinary Perspectives on International Law and International Relations*, Cambridge: Cambridge University Press, 2013.

Fujita, Sanae, 'The challenges of mainstreaming human rights in the World Bank', 5(3) *The International Journal of Human Rights*, March 2011.

Genser, Jared and Irwin Cotler (eds), *The Responsibility to Protect. The Promise of Stopping Mass Atrocities in our Time*, Oxford: Oxford University Press, 2012.

Genugten, Willem van, 'Protection of Indigenous Peoples on the African Continent: Concepts, Position Seeking, and the Interaction of Legal Systems', 104 (1) *American Journal of International Law*, 2010.

Genugten, Willem van, 'The universalisation of human rights: reflections on obstacles and the way forward', in: Sonja Zweegers and Afke de Groot, *Global Values in a Changing World*, Amsterdam: KIT Publishers, 2012.

Genugten, Willem van and Camilo Perez-Bustillo (eds), *The Poverty of Rights; Human Rights and the Eradication of Poverty*, London/New York: Zed Books, 2001.

Genugten, Willem van, Kees Homan, Nico Schrijver and Paul de Waart, *The United Nations of the Future. Globalization with a Human Face*, Amsterdam: KIT Publishers, 2006.

Genugten, Willem van, Mariya Gromilova, Nicola Jägers, Evgeni Moyakine and Laura de Vries, *Company-community Conflicts: The Effectiveness of Outcomes of Non-judicial Conflict Resolution. An Exploratory Report*, report prepared for ACCESS Facility, The Hague, October 2013.

Genugten, Willem van, Nicola Jägers and Evgeni Moyakine, 'Private Military and Security Companies, Transnational Private Regulation and Public International Law: From the Public to the Private and Back Again?', in: Jernej Letnar Černič and Tara Van Ho (eds), *Human Rights and Business: Direct Corporate Accountability for Human Rights*, Oisterwijk: Wolf Legal Publishers, forthcoming (2015).

Genugten, Willem van, Paul Hunt and Susan Mathews (eds), *World Bank, IMF and Human Rights*, Nijmegen: Wolf Legal Publishers, 2003.

Ghazi, Bahram and Shariat Panahi, *The IMF, the World Bank Group and the Question of Human Rights*, New York: Transnational Publishers, 2005.

Gianviti, François, *Economic, Social and Cultural Rights and the International Monetary Fund*, Washington: IMF, 2002.

Gibney, Marc and Sigrun Skogly (eds), *Universal Human Rights and Extraterritorial Obligations*, Philadelphia: University of Pennsylvania Press, 2010.

Goldsmith, Jack, and Eric A. Posner, *The Limits of International Law*, Oxford: Oxford University Press, 2005.

Gondek, Michal, *The Reach of Human Rights in a Globalising World: Extraterritorial Application of Human Rights Treaties*, Antwerp: Intersentia: 2009.

Hakimi, M., 'State Bystander Responsibility', 21(2) *European Journal of International Law*, 2010.

Hallo de Wolf, Antenor, *Reconciling Privatization with Human Rights*, Antwerp: Intersentia, 2011.

Harrison, J., 'Human Rights Measurement: Reflections on the Current Practice and Future Potential of Human Rights Impact Assessment', 13 *Journal of Human Rights Practice* 2, 2011.

Heijer, Maarten den and Rick Lawson, 'Extraterritorial Human Rights and the Concept of "Jurisdiction"', in: Malcolm Langford, Wouter Vandenhole,

Martin Scheinin and Willem van Genugten (eds), *Global Justice, State Duties. The Extraterritorial Scope of Economic, Social and Cultural Rights in International Law*, Cambridge: Cambridge University Press, 2013.

Hert, Paul de and Fisnik Korenica, 'The Doctrine of Equivalent Protection: Its Life and Legitimacy Before and After the European Union's Accession to the European Convention on Human Rights', 13 *German Law Journal*, 2012.

Human Rights Watch, *Abuse-Free Development: How the World Bank Should Safeguard Against Human Rights Violations*, New York, July 2013.

International Commission on Intervention and State Sovereignty, *The Responsibility to Protect*, Report of the International Commission, Ottawa: IDRC, 2001.

Kamminga, Menno T. and Martin Scheinin (eds), *The Impact of Human Rights on General International Law*, Oxford: Oxford University Press, 2009.

Kennedy, John F., School of Government, Cambridge MA, *Rights-Compatible Grievance Mechanisms: A Guidance Tool for Companies and their Stakeholders*, Corporate Social Responsibility Initiative Working Paper No. 41, Cambridge MA: Harvard University, January 2008.

Khalfan, Ashfaq, 'Division of Responsibility amongst States', in: Malcolm Langford, Wouter Vandenhole, Martin Scheinin and Willem van Genugten (eds), *Global Justice, State Duties. The Extraterritorial Scope of Economic, Social and Cultural Rights in International Law*, Cambridge: Cambridge University Press, 2013.

Khalfan, Ashfaq and Ian Seiderman, 'Extraterritorial Human Rights Obligations: Wider Implications of the Maastricht Principles and the Continuing Accountability Challenge', in: Wouter Vandenhole (ed.), *Challenging Territoriality in Human Rights Law: Building Blocks for a Plural and Diverse Duty-Bearer Regime*, Routledge, forthcoming (2015).

Kingsbury, B., 'Operational Policies of International Institutions as Part of the Law-Making Process: The World Bank and Indigenous Peoples', in: Guy Goodwin-Gill and Stefan Talmon (eds), *The Reality of International Law, Essays in Honour of Ian Brownlie*, Oxford: Clarendon Press, 1999.

Kinley, David, *Civilising Globalisation; Human Rights and the Global Economy*, Cambridge: Cambridge University Press, 2009.

Klein, Pierre, 'The Attribution of Conduct to International Organizations', in: James Crawford, Alain Pellet and Simon Olleson (eds), *The Law of International Responsibility*, Oxford: Oxford University Press, 2010.

Langford, Malcolm, Fons Coomans and F. Gómez Isa, 'Extraterritorial Duties in International Law', in: Malcolm Langford, Wouter Vandenhole,

Martin Scheinin and Willem van Genugten (eds), *Global Justice, State Duties. The Extraterritorial Scope of Economic, Social and Cultural Rights in International Law*, Cambridge: Cambridge University Press, 2013.

Letnar Černič, Jernej and Tara Van Ho (eds), *Human Rights and Business: Direct Corporate Accountability for Human Rights*, Oisterwijk: Wolf Legal Publishers, forthcoming (2015).

McBeth, Adam, 'A Right by an Other Name: There Evasive Engagement of International Financial Institutions with Human Rights', 40 *The George Washington International Law Review*, 2009.

McInerney-Lankford, Siobhán and Hans-Otto Sano, *Human Rights Indicators in Development*, Washington: World Bank & the Nordic Trust Fund, 2010.

Ministry of Foreign Affairs of The Netherlands, *Action Plan on Business and Human Rights*, The Hague, April 2014.

Murray, O., 'Piercing the Corporate Veil: The Responsibility of Member States of an International Organization', *International Organizations Law Review*, 8, 2011.

Narula, Smita, 'International Financial Institutions, Transnational Corporations and Duties of States', in: Malcolm Langford, Wouter Vandenhole, Martin Scheinin and Willem van Genugten (eds), *Global Justice, State Duties. The Extraterritorial Scope of Economic, Social and Cultural Rights in International Law*, Cambridge: Cambridge University Press, 2013.

Nordic Trust Fund, *Study on Human Rights Impact Assessments; A Review of the Literature, Differences with other Forms of Assessments and Relevance for Development*, Washington, February 2013.

Oduwole, Olajumoke O., 'International Law and the Right To Development: A Pragmatic Approach For Africa', The Hague: International Institute of Social Studies, 2014.

OECD and World Bank, *Integrating Human Rights into Development: Donor Approaches, Experiences, and Challenges*, 2nd edition, Washington, 2013.

Palacio, Ana, *The Way Forward; Human Rights and the World Bank*, Washington: World Bank Institute, Special Report Development Outreach, 2006.

Rawls, John, *The Law of Peoples*, Cambridge: Harvard University Press, 1999.

Reinisch, August, 'Aid or Assistance and Direction and Control between States and International Organizations in the Commission of Internationally Wrongful Acts', 7 *International Organizations Law Review*, 2010.

Reinisch, A. and J. Wurm, 'International Financial Institutions before National Courts', *International Financial Institutions & International Law*, 2010.

Rombouts, S.J., *Having a Say: Indigenous Peoples, International Law and Free, Prior and Informed Consent*, Oisterwijk: Wolf Legal Publishers, 2014.

Ryngaert, Cedric, 'Jurisdiction: Towards a Reasonableness Test', in: Malcolm Langford, Wouter Vandenhole, Martin Scheinin and Willem van Genugten (eds), *Global Justice, State Duties. The Extraterritorial Scope of Economic, Social and Cultural Rights in International Law*, Cambridge: Cambridge University Press, 2013.

Sachs, Jeffrey D., *Investing in Development. A Practical Plan to Achieve the Millennium Development Goals*, London/Sterling: Earthscan, Millennium Project, United Nations Development Programme, 2005.

Salomon, Margot E., and Colin Arnott, 'Better Development Decision-making: Applying International Human Rights Law to Neoclassical Economics', 32(1) *Nordic Journal of Human Rights*, 2014.

Scheinin, Martin, 'Just Another Word? Jurisdiction in the Roadmaps of State Responsibility and Human Rights', in: Malcolm Langford, Wouter Vandenhole, Martin Scheinin and Willem van Genugten (eds), *Global Justice, State Duties. The Extraterritorial Scope of Economic, Social and Cultural Rights in International Law*, Cambridge: Cambridge University Press, 2013.

Skogly, Sigrun, 'Crimes Against Humanity – revisited: Is there a role for economic and social rights?', 5 *International Journal of Human Rights*, 2001.

Skogly, Sigrun, 'The Human Rights Obligations of the World Bank and the IMF', in: Willem van Genugten, Paul Hunt and Susan Mathews (eds), *World Bank, IMF and Human Rights*, Nijmegen: Wolf Legal Publishers, 2003.

Skogly, Sigrun, *Beyond National Borders: States' Human Rights Obligations in International Cooperation*, Antwerp: Intersentia, 2006.

Skogly, Sigrun, 'Causality and Extraterritorial Human Rights Obligations', in: Malcolm Langford, Wouter Vandenhole, Martin Scheinin and Willem van Genugten (eds), *Global Justice, State Duties. The Extraterritorial Scope of Economic, Social and Cultural Rights in International Law*, Cambridge: Cambridge University Press, 2013.

Slaughter, Anne-Marie, *A New World Order*, Princeton/Oxford: Princeton University Press, 2004.

Spijkers, Otto, *The United Nations, the Evolution of Global Values and International Law*, Cambridge/Antwerp/Portland: Intersentia, 2011.

Staden, Alfred van, *Between the Rule of Power and the Power of Rule. In Search of an Effective World Order*, Leiden/Boston: Martinus Nijhoff, 2007.
Stiglitz, Joseph E., *Globalization and its Discontents*, New York/London: W.W. Norton & Company, 2002.
Tzevelekos, Vassilis, 'Revisiting the Humanisation of International Law: Limits and Potential - Obligations Erga Omnes, Hierarchy of Rules and the Principle of Due Diligence as the Basis for Further Humanisation', 6(1) *Erasmus Law Review*, 2013.
United Nations Development Programme, *Human Development Report 2011, Sustainability and Equity: A Better Future for All*, Oxford: Oxford University Press, 2012.
Vandenbogaerde, Arne, 'The Right to Development in International Human Rights Law: A Call for its Dissolution', 31(2) *Netherlands Quarterly of Human Rights*, 2013.
Vandenhole, Wouter, 'EU and Development: Extraterritorial Obligations under the ICESCR', in: Margot Salomon, Arne Tostensen and Wouter Vandenhole (eds), *Casting the Net Wider: Human Rights, Development and New Duty-Bearers*, Antwerp/Oxford: Intersentia, 2007.
Vandenhole, Wouter (ed.), *Challenging Territoriality in Human Rights Law: Building Blocks for a Plural and Diverse Duty-Bearer Regime*, Routledge, forthcoming (2015).
World Bank Institute, *Public-Private Partnerships Reference Guide*, Washington, April 2012.
World Bank and IMF, *Global Monitoring Reports*, Washington: World Bank, 2004–2013.
World Commission on the Social Dimension of Globalization, *A Fair Globalization; Creating Opportunities for All*, Geneva: International Labour Organization, 2004
Wouters, J. and C. Ryngaert, 'Good Governance in International Organisations', in: D. Curtin and R. Wessel (eds), *Good Governance and the European Union. Reflections on Concepts, Institutions and Substance*, Antwerp: Intersentia, 2005.

www.ingramcontent.com/pod-product-compliance
Ingram Content Group UK Ltd.
Pitfield, Milton Keynes, MK11 3LW, UK
UKHW021843100926
8556IPUK00019B/1024

9 781780 682969